BANISH BOREDOM

Activities to Do with Kids That You'll ACTUALLY Enjoy

Rebecca Green

Gryphon House
www.gryphonhouse.com

Published by Gryphon House, Inc.
P. O. Box 10, Lewisville, NC 27023
800.638.0928; 877.638.7576 (fax)
Visit us on the web at www.gryphonhouse.com.

Photographs courtesy of Rebecca Green.

Bulk Purchase

Gryphon House books are available for special premiums and sales promotions as well as for fund-raising use. Special editions or book excerpts also can be created to specifications. For details, call 800.638.0928.

Disclaimer

Gryphon House, Inc., cannot be held responsible for damage, mishap, or injury incurred during the use of or because of activities in this book. Appropriate and reasonable caution and adult supervision of children involved in activities and corresponding to the age and capability of each child involved are recommended at all times. When making choices about allowing children to participate in activities with certain ingredients, make sure to investigate possible toxicity and consider any food allergies or sensitivities. Do not leave children unattended at any time. Observe safety and caution at all times.

Library of Congress Cataloging-in-Publication Data

The Cataloging-in-Publication Data is registered with the Library of Congress for 978-0-87659-345-5.

DEDICATION

To Kane and Cameron, my "always up for an adventure" loves who embrace wholeheartedly the idea of always saying yes and never being bored. To my husband who puts up with my never-ending shenanigans and our creative mess, and exemplifies with gusto the value of hard work and unconditional love. And to my parents, for nurturing creativity and an endless set of interests, and supporting me no matter what.

CONTENTS

INTRODUCTION

Hello! If you're picking up this book, I'm guessing that (like me) you are a parent who has spent some time wondering what you are supposed to do with your children now that they are no longer babies who sleep, coo, or cry most of the day. Now they're just as cute (most of the time), but they are verbal, mobile, and ready to explore. You're looking for some activities that will keep them stimulated, contribute to their physical and intellectual growth, and that you can enjoy and participate in as well. It can be a difficult balance!

As a mom of two young children, I have gone through the exact same transition, and I started writing a blog to share how I deal with the challenges. This book is based on my personal experiences and my realization that the best activities parents can share with young children take into account the personalities of both the parent and child. It's incredibly easy to lose yourself and your own identity when you become a parent, and that can especially be a concern if you leave a career outside the home to raise your children as I did. But I've found that as our kids have grown, the most enjoyable activities we do together started from something that I was interested in myself and then adapted to best fit the developing personalities of each of our children.

I am actually an attorney by education and trade, and for several years I practiced law as an attorney in a so-called "big-law" firm. But after having our two children, it started to become clear that, for me, I wouldn't be able to be both the attorney and mom that I wanted to be. So I decided to take a break from practicing law and stay at home with our children while they were young.

When my family and I decided that I would stay home full-time, I knew that I needed a plan. So I pulled out all of the old calendars from our kids' fabulous day care and tried to put together my own themed monthly plan. And I felt better. But by the second or third day of being a stay-at-home mom (SAHM), I realized that I had planned our entire days without much consideration of what the kids or I might actually like to do. I had gone the cookie-cutter-lesson-plan route, which seemed to contradict part of the reason I was staying home with them in the first place.

I recall frantically Googling, "What do I do with my kids?" in the early morning hours that first week home and discovering the creative parent blogs. (These are commonly called "mommy blogs," but dads publish good blogs too!) I found blogs full of really creative art projects, science experiments, and visits to local destinations. I was relieved and remember thinking to myself, "I can do this!"

And I did. We jumped into adventures, and I started writing about them almost immediately—first in a small family blog. Then I moved to the more public realm with our Not-So-SAHM blog (http://www.notsosahm.blogspot.com), whose name reflects our tendency to get out and explore rather than staying at home. I found a sense of accomplishment in documenting what we had done and maintaining my writing skills, a joy in establishing connections with other parents doing similar things, and some accountability to find new activities and follow through on them. I drew on my own creative childhood, which was filled with art, crafts, science, and outdoor activities. I planned some activities with the kids ahead of time and let others develop more organically. I consider myself quite lucky that I began staying home when the weather was nice outside—and that we live in a city with plenty of free and fantastic activities. I also know my entire family is lucky that I'm able to stay home at all.

> Besides the activities I plan, I also make sure my children have plenty of free play time by themselves, which is an important skill all on its own.

We were busy those first six months or so, before the kids were in school. As they've both transitioned to longer days at school and organized extracurricular activities, the amount and kinds of things we do together has certainly changed. Besides the activities I plan, I also make sure my children have plenty of free play time by themselves, which is an important skill all on its own. But we've been so fortunate through all of our experiences together, developing and growing along the way. From those experiences, I have gained a sense of what types of activities are fun and educational for the kids and at the same time provide fulfillment for me as a parent and a person. Given how helpful I found other parent resources when I started staying home, I felt that sharing what I have learned would be useful to other parents. I may be at home full-time right now, but any parent, whether working outside the home full-time or part-time, or at home full-time, can use the resources in this book.

The Personal Approach to Activities

I know that as parents, we are often looking for "the answer" to our numerous questions about raising our children. But my overarching point in this book is to find your own approach to activities with your children—one that suits your personality as you help your children discover their own. That might seem obvious, but it was something I first overlooked. That's the humbling point about being a parent: even the brightest, most well-intentioned people (including you, of course) have no idea what to do when taking on this new role. But through some trial and error, I've arrived at an approach that works well for us. My personal goal with all the activities I do with our children is to help them become well-rounded people by exposing them to a variety of different disciplines and to encourage them to become creative, confident, and independent thinkers who can question critically and work through issues.

The question is, where do you start? I've had the best success by starting with myself. Ask yourself, what things do I want to explore or learn more about? Pick one and start there. And then watch as your children react to activities involving that interest. I'm going to guess that as a parent of young kids, you're thinking something along the lines of: "Coffee. Coffee is something I can get into." If so, find a local roaster and take the kids for a field trip! Maybe they'll be enamored by machinery, maybe they'll enjoy the smell, or maybe you'll come up with an art project out of coffee grounds. Or maybe you'll just get an amazing cup of coffee out of it.

I continue to be surprised at how quickly I can tell what kinds of things are going to appeal to each of our children's personalities, which allows me to come up with slight variations on each activity that will suit each child. For example, even though both of our kids love exploring, our daughter, Cameron, is more of a directions follower than our son, Kane, who really likes flexibility and creativity. They both love geocaching, which involves treasure-hunting using a website and a navigation device to guide you. Cameron, however, is more focused on the mechanics of following the Global Positioning System (GPS) device to find the treasure, and Kane likes to know the story behind the geocaches placed there by other treasure-hunting enthusiasts. So I try to satisfy each interest as we do the same activity—Cam helps me use the GPS to track the geocache while Kane and I think through the clues and the story behind the placement. And if one sibling doesn't like a particular activity and the other does, it's a good opportunity to teach the lesson that sometimes you need to be flexible, compromise, and be patient while the other person gets a turn at what they like.

Having trouble picking an activity that you think is suitable? My second piece of advice is not to underestimate your kids. I generally try to stretch our children to do activities that might be labeled as slightly above their age, or maybe even something you may not initially think would be an activity for children. For example, I took our children (age four and five at the time) to tour the Library of Congress, which solicited some surprised reactions from friends. And upon arrival, a library docent told me that the tour was generally advised for children at least eight years old. But we stayed, and although they may not have experienced the hour-long tour the same way an older child or adult would have, they did learn something. They learned to be polite, wait patiently, listen carefully, ask questions of adults, and so on. And they even picked up some new knowledge along the way. I try to always remind myself that with all activities, it's about the process and not the product. They didn't come out of that tour as historical scholars, but they learned a lot in the process. It doesn't always work out—our children are still children and we've had our fair share of fabulous, dramatic exits—but in my opinion, the more we do these kinds of activities, the better children get at doing them and the more they get out of them each successive time.

My last piece of advice is to do your research but stay flexible. You may have found the perfect morning music concert to attend, but on your way there, you walk past a construction site and it turns out your kids would like to sit on a dirty curb for hours watching construction vehicles.

Try to roll with it. I've found that sometimes unplanned activities work out the best. If I'm too focused on a particular goal I have in mind, I might miss an opportunity to discover something our kids would enjoy more. On a related note, don't worry if something doesn't turn out the way you planned—the kids probably won't even notice. And if they do care about plans being changed, it's another life lesson learned—we all need to learn to adapt to changing plans. (It's probably telling that one of our family's favorite songs is "You Can't Always Get What You Want.") As your children get older, you'll find that they're able to communicate more clearly about the kinds of things they like to do, and you can solicit their help in choosing and adapting activities.

To sum up my approach:

- **Start with activities you like.** Your toddler probably can't tell a Monet from a Lichtenstein but might like climbing stairs. So a trip to an art museum where the kids get to stretch their legs and you get an art fix and a decent cup of coffee is a perfect place to start. Plus I've found that if I'm excited or interested in doing a particular activity, our kids are more likely to be excited and interested as well.

- **Consider your own personality.** I know that parents can feel a lot of pressure to participate in certain kinds of activities with their kids, but I don't think there is anything wrong with taking into account your own personality when choosing things to do with your children. I've found that it's good to stretch myself a bit and try activities I might be hesitant about doing. But if you're a homebody and force yourself to plan major outings daily, at the end of the day you're likely to wind up being an unhappy parent and, in turn, probably having an unhappy child.

- **Adapt activities to your child's interests and personality.** Find something about each activity that appeals to each of your children and focus on that. Even if it's not an activity that your children are interested in initially, working with them to find something about it that they like exposes them to something new, while showing them how to think outside the box a bit.

ART PROJECTS

When I first started staying home, I found that it was incredibly easy to fall into a trap of planning all our activities around our kids without much, if any, consideration of the things that I like to do. Given that they were so young (ages one and two and a half), that meant planning typical kid activities around their nap schedules, mealtimes, bathroom trips, and so on. It's a natural thing to do and it makes sense. But I felt like I was starting to lose myself just a little bit, and I came to the realization that it was perfectly fine to plan some things to do with the kids that I liked too. And art was one of those areas in which I first started to make that transition.

When the first few art projects (such as cutting shapes out of paper) were not provoking the kind of creativity I was aiming for, I realized that my focus should be more on the art of making—in other words, putting process over product. The kids and I started undertaking more open-ended art projects. Even though they don't always end up as frame-worthy pieces, we all enjoy the process so much more. My general approach is to give the kids freedom to create how they want—even within the confines of a particular project. For example, I might pick the particular art media we use, such as watercolors, but have them decide what they want to do with it. Or I might have a more focused project, such as creating pop art of themselves for Father's Day, but let them pick their own colors. I love watching the kids make choices, figure out how and what they want to do, and follow the paths down which their creativity takes them. By exposing them to activities I enjoy, they've started to develop their own interests. But I still have fun and stay interested. And that gives me more satisfaction at the end of the day, and in turn, I think makes it a better experience for our kids as well.

Preparing for Art Making

Before gathering materials, I find that it's helpful to spend some time thinking about what kind of art you'd like to make with your kids. To come up with project ideas, I think about the kind of art I enjoyed making when I was young, spend time researching ideas online, and peruse kid art blogs and books. We have been inspired by art we see on our field trips and sometimes think of our own projects based on those observations, but I generally have a running list of art projects we'd like to try.

If you first gather ideas about the kind of art you'd like to make, then you can more easily find ways to purchase art supplies cost-effectively. You can save by buying in bulk, so I try to use the same materials for several different projects. After our art supplies were pretty well stocked, I found it much easier to set the kids up with simple activities, such as just coloring with markers. (See the Resources section for our list of favorite art suppliers.)

As you can tell, it's also important to consider the age of your children and their particular personalities before choosing a project. I always try to choose projects that both of my children can participate in, even if it's in a slightly different way. For example, we did a spray-painted coffee filters project that was well suited for my oldest, Kane, who had developed enough motor skills to physically squeeze a bottle full of watercolors. Cameron wasn't quite at that stage, but she was perfectly capable of using a paintbrush to achieve a similar effect. I let her try using the squeeze bottle but had the backup available so she could still participate and not get frustrated.

I know that there are some projects one of our kids will enjoy more than the other, but I encourage both to try. I also offer options that might better suit their particular personalities. We certainly have moments when one decides not to participate, and I don't force them. But I find that they have a hard time not joining once we get started.

Cameron has an affinity for painting on her body instead of on whatever traditional media we're using, so I quickly learned to set up workspaces to allow her to do that. I once taped large sheets of paper to the wall around their bathtub and set them up with brushes and glow-in-the-dark paint. I have a portable black light that I plugged in far away from the tub and obviously kept the tub empty for safety. Kane went right to work painting on the paper, but all Cam wanted to do was paint herself from head to toe. When they were done, all I had to do was take down the paper and run the tub.

I've also found it's helpful to try to keep a laid-back attitude toward art and mess (which doesn't always work). By now, it should be fairly obvious that I don't mind a little mess. But if the idea of having a fully painted child run down the hallway or having glitter strewn throughout your living room strikes fear in your heart, then don't do it! Find a project that is creative and fits your comfort level. It's not going to be fun for anyone if you have to obsessively sweep under your child's chair throughout the whole project.

Once you have the materials and an idea of what project you and your kids would like to do, make sure you think through how much time you'll need for the project; no one likes to be rushed. I also like to set up the art project area, gather the materials, and then spend some time talking to my kids about what we're going to do. If a project needs to be done in stages, don't put out all of the materials at once. You'll just get frustrated when the kids inevitably go straight to stage four. I also occasionally show my kids examples of a finished project, when available, particularly if we are trying to create in the style of a certain artist. But I generally like to try to keep their minds open and not make them feel like they have to create in a certain way.

To that end, I sometimes join in, but have found that when I do, my kids frequently try to imitate what I'm doing or ask me to do things for them. So more often, I just sit with them and talk about what they're doing or wherever else our conversation leads. I'm also perfectly comfortable setting them up with an easy project and doing something else nearby. Although

I'd love to do art all day, I also use it as a time to keep them occupied while I need to get other things done. I've had several stern conversations with the dishes, but they still appear incapable of washing themselves.

Art Project Ideas

As I mentioned earlier, I like to have a list of projects handy when we need an idea to get us started. These are our favorites, with additional options noted for some activities. As you gather materials on the lists, make sure you have enough for all children participating. You can adjust each project to best suit your child's age and temperament, but most of them we've done in some form since Cam was one year old. (Remember: Don't underestimate them!)

BIG PAINTING

Both of our kids love to get messy while making art. In fact, I often set them up for art projects in swimsuits because I know that whatever they're doing, it's going to be all over them. And big painting might be their favorite messy art project for that very reason. On top of the good fun, I love big painting because it helps develop

PAINT CHOICES

We love to use BioColor paint, which retains the individual paint colors when mixed and scraped together more than regular tempera paint. But mixing colors is also another important skill, so regular tempera paint is fine too.

gross and fine motor skills, teaches them a bit about restraint (in terms of how much paint to use), and stimulates creative storytelling for them.

They are both big fans of making up stories about what they're painting as they are painting it. I'm not sure if it's because this is such an active way of making art or because of the fluid nature of the media, but when they move the paint around with the scraper, the paint seems to come alive for them. Our kids view the paint as doing something while they create art and often describe the paint as actual physical matter—like water or lava—that is working to create a scene (such as an ocean with a deserted island). They envision people or animals moving around in that scene (George Washington might be storming that deserted island). This is a great activity to let the kids work on by themselves, and big art can take big time, which can be a nice break for me. However, I find it hard not to get sucked into the stories they are telling! But giving them the license ahead of time to make a total mess takes the stress out of the activity for everyone and is so much more fun.

Materials

- Several colors of tempera paint in squeezable bottles
- A large piece of canvas or sturdy poster board
- A paint squeegee or scraper, an old credit card, or a sturdy piece of thin cardboard

Directions

1. Set up the canvas or poster board so your children can reach the entire piece or can easily turn it to reach the entire media area.

2. Provide several colors of paint and let your children squeeze it onto the canvas, scraping it around in whatever pattern they like. Encourage them to start with a small amount of paint until they get a sense of how much is too much.

3. Let the painting dry well, and then hang it as abstract art; use it as a play board for other toy setup, storytelling, or play acting, or save it to cut into cards for friends and family.

I like to encourage my children to talk to me about what they are painting while they are scraping. (When it comes to talking, my kids don't need a lot of encouragement!) But if your child prefers to paint in silence, that's fine too. I can tell that sometimes they just need some quiet time to think while they're painting. You can also try playing music or an audiobook and see if they enjoy painting with that in the background instead.

Additional Options

- Using nontoxic paints, place a large piece of poster board or a white sheet of paper on the ground and let your littlest ones paint using their entire body. This works best in a diaper or bathing suit, and probably outside.

- Use a variety of big brushes (hand broom, sponges, and so on) to paint whatever canvas you're working on.
- Get a group together to work collectively on a big painting mural. We like to do this outdoors and hang up a large piece of paper or a white sheet. It's so interesting to see how kids collaborate to make a joint piece of art!

BLEEDING ART TISSUE PAPER PAINTING

Although its name is a bit unfortunate, bleeding art tissue paper creates some of the most beautiful art and is a big favorite of our children. Part of the fun is they get to make a total mess before the painting even starts (by ripping up large sheets of tissue paper into smaller shapes). There is also an element of surprise because you're never entirely sure how the painting is going to turn out until it dries. This type of art project gets better and better as it progresses. Plus it results in a gorgeous product with so many uses. I always make sure to participate in this one and am often found at the art table by myself long after the kids have moved on. We have years' worth of bleeding art tissue paper gift tags from our efforts.

Materials
- Several colors of bleeding art tissue paper (not regular tissue paper)
- Thick watercolor paper
- Paintbrushes
- Water
- Children's scissors (optional)
- Glue (optional)

Directions
1. Start by having your children rip or cut the large tissue paper into smaller pieces. I like the look that using torn paper creates. But if your kids love using scissors or if you're going for a cleaner look, then let them cut the paper into shapes. Have them separate the pieces into piles by color. The paper is easier to use once they get going and they get to work on their color recognition.

2. Brush a little water onto the watercolor paper, place a piece of tissue paper on it, and paint over it with more water. The wetter the tissue paper gets, the more the colors will bleed and mix into each other. Resist removing the tissue paper just yet.

3. When your children are happy with the shapes they've made, let the painting dry. Then, have them pull away the tissue paper pieces to reveal the painting made underneath! (Tip: Save those pieces of tissue paper—you can reuse them!) Hang the painting as is, cut it into pieces and attach it to a string to make a pretty garland, or cover it with contact paper to make a unique place mat.

Additional Options

- Paint the tissue paper as a sun catcher onto a window, door, or clear easel. Let dry for temporary art and remove and rinse when finished.

- Reuse pieces of tissue paper for collages or to simulate stained glass by pressing the tissue pieces onto a piece of clear contact paper and then hanging the artwork in a window.

- Instead of using water, paint tissue paper onto paper using a water and glue mixture. Less light will come through, but the colors will be brighter. Or paint them onto an empty plastic bottle to make a cool lantern. (You can see an example on the blog; search for "tissue paper bottle lights.")

MULTIMEDIA COLLAGE

Collage can be one of the best open-ended art projects for kids. To start, this type of project can help you and your children reuse the vast piles of other art that they've created but that you haven't been able to toss. I start with this old artwork and add in a few standard supplies, and then I always love to throw in something unusual to see what creative use they'll come up with. Striped pipe cleaners become animal tails, buttons become building blocks, and so on. Sometimes our kids make three-dimensional collages and vertically build a sculpture upward. And sometimes they create collages that are flat depictions of things. Try to resist asking what they're making—it doesn't have to be anything, really. You just never know what kids are going to come up with when you give them simple supplies and little or no direction.

Materials

- Thick cardboard cut into medium-sized rectangular pieces (about 6" x 9")—big enough to provide an ample collage area without creating something too heavy that will break

- A variety of collage materials—I like to recycle other art, such as pieces of a big painting, into collage supplies. I also like to include some tactile, manipulative supplies, such as textured foil paper or pipe cleaners. And Cam always likes something shiny too.

- Children's scissors strong enough to cut the collage materials (Or you can cut them in advance for younger children.)
- Brush-top bottles filled with glue or small containers of glue and paintbrushes

Directions

Give each child a piece of cardboard, a brush, and make sure the glue and collage materials are within reach. Let them go, and see what they create!

Additional Options

- Talk to your children about geometric mosaics and have them try making them with collage materials, creating a shape or a repeating color pattern.
- Have your child draw something and then fill it in with collage pieces.
- Collect items from nature or your pantry (for example, beans or pasta) and let the children use them to make organic collages.
- Make animal or monster collages using shapes and photos cut from magazines. (See an example on the blog by searching for "monster collages.")
- For older children working on letter and number recognition, provide a drawing that you've divided into sections and labeled with letters or numbers. Make a corresponding color code for the sections (for example, use red materials for *A* and purple materials for *B*) and have the children create a mosaic by number or letter.

PAINT PRINTMAKING

The thing I love most about printmaking with paint is that it is incredibly easy to adapt the project for pretty much any age. Even toddlers can paint with fingerpaints (or even edible fingerpaints for the youngest ones) onto a surface and have an adult help them press paper to their painting to make a print. Plus older children can learn to make prints of more elaborate paintings they make. And, no big surprise, my kids love it in any form because it's generally a messy activity.

In addition, there's just something about being able to reproduce artwork in the form of printmaking that makes kids feel like real grown-up artists. When Kane was in prekindergarten, he decided that he was going to have a school fund-raiser with his fictional band, Team Kaboom. He and Cami (also a band member) wanted to make flyers for their event and hang them at school. Making prints was an excellent, low-tech way to make sure that all the flyers had at least the same background print (he wrote the fund-raiser information on each one himself). I was just trying to encourage his creativity and social consciousness but later learned that he really thought he was going to host the fund-raiser and had started inviting kids and teachers at school. In his mind, the flyers were real, and he was not happy to find out that we were hosting no such event.

Materials

- Fingerpaints or tempera paints
- A hard, clean surface on which to paint—this can be a table, a place mat, the back of an old baking sheet, or even a sheet of acrylic

- Cotton swabs

- A brayer, foam roller, or sponge (With a sponge, which our kids like, you'll need to work a little harder to get an even layer of paint.)

- Thick paper

- A styrofoam tray (optional)

- A pen (optional)

Directions

1. Place a small amount of paint on your surface and use the brayer to spread the paint into a thin layer. (Don't worry about using a brayer if your youngest are doing basic fingerpainting; they'll spread the paint around as they go.)

2. Let your children paint whatever they like, using either their fingers or cotton swabs as a brush.

3. Press a piece of paper on top of the painting, smoothing lightly over the surface.

4. Lift and see your print! Repeat by pressing with additional pieces of paper until the print is no longer clear.

Additional Options

- Try printmaking with colored paper and black paint.

- Have older children sign and number their prints from each limited edition (for example: 15/20, Kane Green) as an artist would do.

- Recycle Styrofoam trays to use as a printmaking surface for slightly older children. Use a pen to scratch an image into the foam, roll the paint over it, and then press the paper on top.

SIDEWALK CHALK PAINT

The kids and I loved doing this art activity when they were very young. Perhaps it's because it instantly brings me back to the wonderfulness of summer, but I also think it's because they were so completely and totally engrossed in getting messy with their art projects. It was really something to watch! I'd seen several different recipes for cornstarch sidewalk paint, and I decided to make it a thick consistency and see what the kids would do with it. I made several colors and gave both children small plastic cups of each to avoid competition and complaints of hogging.

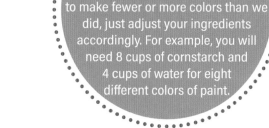

ADJUST FOR THE COLORS

Our recipe generally uses a 2:1 ratio of cornstarch to water, so if you'd like to make fewer or more colors than we did, just adjust your ingredients accordingly. For example, you will need 8 cups of cornstarch and 4 cups of water for eight different colors of paint.

Materials

- 6 cups cornstarch
- 3 cups water
- 6 colors of washable tempera paint

Directions

1. Working with one batch at a time, in a medium bowl, mix together 1 cup cornstarch with 1/2 cup water. Stir until the cornstarch is incorporated well. It will take a little muscle; the kids typically like to help with this.

2. Add several drops of one color of tempera paint. If you'd like the color to be brighter, add a little more. Mix until you get your desired color. Then transfer the colored paint to a smaller container for painting.

3. Repeat until you have six different colors of paint (or as many as you like).

4. Once you have all the sidewalk paint mixed, take your kids outside, hand it over, and watch out. We first did this project when the kids were really young (one and two-and-a-half years old). My children started off making small dribbles with paintbrushes onto the sidewalk, and they soon moved to pouring it out in big globs all over each other. Although I wished I had put the kids in their bathing suits, I encouraged their inclination to turn the art project into a sensory experience. They squished and swirled colors together and loved it so much that neither seemed bothered by the fact that they were being covered with a sticky mess. A plus of taking messy art outdoors is the actual cleanup itself. When you hose them down, the kids also think it's bonus water play. Don't worry; it washes out—even out of hair.

Additional Options

- Help your kids use the chalk paint to mark outdoor games, such as hopscotch or tic-tac-toe.

- Hit the streets and chalk-mark around your neighborhood. Consider your neighbors and use your discretion! Someone on our street wrote "Look both ways!" on every corner, and I loved it. But not everyone will appreciate such things.

- Use the paint as a fun opportunity to practice and reinforce letters and numbers by having the kids trace templates you've already marked on the sidewalk.

SPRAY-PAINTING ART

I'm all for keeping art projects simple, but something special happens when you hand your children each a spray bottle. You think they like glue? Watch their reaction when you give them a bottle full of paint and tell them to start spraying. They can't stop. This can be a very messy project—but it's worth it. It helps kids learn a variety of skills, including gross and fine motor skills, eye-hand coordination, and restraint (too much watery paint will rip the paper). Plus it is just an interesting, out-of-the-ordinary art project, and they'll love watching the different colors spread and diffuse throughout the filter.

The first time we tried this project, Kane kept going and going until we ran out of filters. He was a little man on a mission. But Cameron didn't quite have the coordination or strength to squeeze the handle of the bottle herself yet. Of course she didn't want any help, so I watched as she determinedly shook the spray bottle over the coffee filter to get the paint out. It worked, but she wasn't exactly getting the result she wanted. She eventually took the paintbrush and cup of watercolors I offered and painted away, happy to join in the project. She can now squeeze the bottle handle with the best of them, but it was important at that time for me to adapt the project for her so she didn't get frustrated. Even if you don't think about it beforehand, be willing to change a project so that it works well for each child's age.

<u>Materials</u>

For each child:

- A small spray bottle

- Coffee filters (High-quality paper works best.)

- Liquid watercolors (washable preferred)

- A drop cloth or kraft paper

<u>Directions</u>

1. Choose a work area knowing that paint will travel a short distance, and cover the area with a drop cloth or kraft paper.

2. Have older children help fill several spray bottles with different colors of liquid watercolors. (I like to do the fill-up over a container, which catches any overflow.)

3. Place coffee filters out on the work area, and let the kids spray away!

<u>Additional Options</u>

- Is the thought of spraying paint inside your home making you break out in hives? Take it outside! Use the coffee filters, or hang up an old bedsheet or roll of paper and let your kids spray a big mural.

- Skip the paint altogether, and turn this activity into an art and science project. Use markers to color the coffee filters with a design. Then spray plain water onto the filters and watch the colors spread into a pretty watercolor look.

- You will undoubtedly find yourself with lots and lots of watercolored filters. Save them and string them together (either in a vertical stack or horizontally) to make an easy party garland.

SPIN ART

I recall playing with a tiny spin-art machine when I was a young girl and being totally mesmerized by the gorgeous images that came into focus as the paper stopped spinning. There is something so magical about the result. However, as an adult, I'm routinely disappointed by the limits such prefabricated artistic gadgets present. I was incredibly excited to find projects using salad spinners to create the same effect. (You can find them at inexpensive prices.) Besides loving the element of surprise involved in spin art, children love the act of spinning itself—whirling the handle around faster and faster to get the paint to spin, and tinkering with paint amount, placement, and colors to achieve different results. Plus while mixing paint colors can often result in a lot of brown, spinning the colors almost always yields an amazingly multicolored end product. Of course, the product isn't necessarily the point, but this one can be really fun for kids who get easily frustrated if they don't make something they deem pretty. Think beyond the spinner, and work favorite stories into the activity. Our kids like to assign characters to certain colors and have them battle to see what color spins out on top.

Materials

- A salad spinner (The ones with a hand crank instead of a pull cord work best.)
- Heavy-weight paper or poster board, cut into a size that will fit and lie relatively flat in the spinner
- Squeezable tempera paints (If you can't find prepackaged squeezable paints, mini condiment bottles make great paint containers.)
- Glitter (optional)
- Alternatives to paper, such as egg cartons or fabric (optional)

Directions

1. Have the children place the piece of paper into the bottom of the spinner.
2. Let them squeeze different colors of paint onto the paper, first trying out just a few drops of several colors, and then adding more or less to achieve their desired result.
3. Put the top on and let them crank away! Once the spinner has safely stopped moving, open the top to reveal the painting.

Additional Options

- Add some sparkle to your spinner by sprinkling in glitter after you add the paint. It will mix and dry with the paint to create a really pretty effect.

- Try a medium other than paper. We've used poster board heart cutouts and egg carton cups to make some really neat spin art. And I'd love to try to get an effect similar to tie-dyeing by spinning fabric paint onto fabric.

- In place of a salad spinner, create spin art by putting dots of paint on a round paper plate, turning it over on a piece of paper, and manually turning the plate to put the paint on the paper.

SQUISH PAINTING

We are obsessed with squish painting in our home, and it's absolutely one of the most requested art projects from our kids. Similar to printmaking and spin art, the kids love the element of surprise in making each painting. You can try to plan out a design, but you never really know until after it's been squished what the finished art will look like. In my opinion, the fun process also happens to make some of the most gift-worthy, sophisticated art pieces (especially if you use metallic paint à la Andy Warhol's Rorschach prints). Whenever we break out this project, our entire living room floor is soon covered in a quilt of squish paintings left out to dry. Once the kids get going, they don't want to stop! Cami likes to look at the entire painting as one object or pattern (such as a butterfly or an airplane), whereas Kane likes to interpret it as a scene (frequently involving the defense and attack of some structure). Any way you look at it, they both have fun!

- Medium-weight paper

- Squeezable tempera paints (If you can't find prepackaged squeezable paints, small condiment bottles make great paint containers.)

Directions

4. Have the child fold the paper in half lengthwise so that a crease runs vertically from top to bottom. (This also helps children visualize the line of symmetry.) You can also prefold paper for very young kids.

5. Open the paper to lay it flat again, and allow kids to squeeze paints into whatever pattern they'd like. Sometimes ours try to make matching patterns on each side of the fold; sometimes they paint all over the whole paper randomly.

6. Fold the piece of paper closed, using the prepainting fold for guidance. Let your child squish and smooth the paper shut. Then open to see the finished design!

Additional Options

- Try folding twice for a really unexpected result. After prefolding the paper vertically, fold it in half again along the width, creating four quadrants when you unfold the paper. After painting, fold along one line of symmetry to squish the paint. Open and refold along the second line.

- Add accessories, such as eyes or mustaches, to make monsters, dragons, animals, silly faces, and more!

- Spend some time examining a dried painting with your child and try to pick out shapes and pictures. Use a dark marker or pen to outline the shapes.

- Use the paintings as background art pages to write your own storybook.

TAPE-RESIST PAINTING

Next to glue, tape is the most popular art supply in our home. I honestly can't make much sense out of it, but both kids get so excited if I say we are doing a project using tape. And letting them tear the pieces themselves is a must. So not surprisingly, they both love to make tape-resist painting, and they have ever since they were very young. Plus if you're looking for a time-consuming project, you can absolutely count on this one for the additional time it takes the kids to untape themselves after getting inevitably tangled as they work. Sometimes it's the little things about a project that make it so special.

We first tried our hand at tape-resist painting with watercolors when Cami was about a year old. Since the kids not only like to tear the pieces of tape to use themselves but also like to remove the tape pieces once they've finished painting, they ended up tearing a lot of holes in the paper during the process. Cameron immediately got upset when she "ruined" her art, but Kane took it in stride and decided that the rips and holes were part of the art. (You end up learning a lot about your children's personalities during many of these projects.)

Years later, we visited an exhibit on destructive art at Chicago's Museum of Contemporary Art, which made both of them feel better that such a process could be an intentional way of making art. The first time we tried the tape-resist painting, though, was a good learning opportunity for me to recognize their different personalities and preferences. I realized that I could help Cameron learn to wait to remove the tape until the painting had dried a bit and we could pull it off slowly together. And it was good for Kane to see how to do it without being destructive. But he also knew that if he wanted to tear holes in his painting, that was fine. In my opinion, there is no wrong way to make art, and this was a great project for showing the kids that.

Materials

- Heavy-weight white paper
- Tempera or watercolor paints
- Washi tape (or similar, light-adhesive tape that can be removed easily—painter's tape is a good alternative)
- Glue, white crayon, or chalk (optional)

Directions

1. Have the kids tear pieces of tape in advance and then stick the tape pieces to the paper in whatever design they wish.

2. Allow the kids to paint over the taped paper, encouraging them to cover the white space (so that the resist pattern actually shows up).

3. Let the painting dry almost completely, and then let your children (with appropriate assistance given their age and temperament) remove the tape pieces to reveal the resist!

Additional Options

- Instead of making a random pattern, use the tape to outline a more realistic shape.

- Use the negative space from the tape to write a message and turn the painting into a card for someone special.

- Try other forms of resist painting, using glue, white crayon, or white chalk to draw a design or image. Then paint over it (once dried, for the glue) to reveal the resist.

SCIENCE PROJECTS

Your kids have probably already unknowingly conducted science projects by leaving snacks in their bags for an extended period of time. The periodic emptying of kids' backpacks tends to yield fantastic science experiment results. See, science is already infused into so many everyday activities! Once you start looking, you will have fun pointing out where science is involved in your activities and incorporating it into more projects you do at home. As you've surely experienced, most children constantly want to know why and how, and science is the perfect way to answer so many of their questions (and perhaps, unintentionally even, spur on new ones). Science projects also help children develop important educational and life skills, such as how to make predictions, analyze information, persevere to find answers, and clean up disastrous messes.

Unlike all of the open-ended projects we love, most science experiments typically have a desired outcome—a particular scientific principle I'm trying to teach the kids. I try not to share the anticipated results ahead of time. Instead, we read books and talk about the concepts in advance so they have an idea of what might happen (for example, how mixing various types of liquids will illustrate density). But I let them come up with their own hypotheses and see what happens. Sometimes they develop additional projects based on what we're doing, and I try to be flexible. If you use your imagination a bit, when you need to you can turn the activity into something that better suits your kids at that particular moment.

Preparing for Science Projects

From a young age, our kids have loved all kinds of dress-up play. So I tend to use it as a way to entice them to try activities when they're reluctant. Are your children scared of swimming? Let them dress as scuba divers and go explore. If the idea of chemistry doesn't sound exciting enough, get them lab coats, safety goggles, and real science notebooks to record their observations. Then watch them line up at your designated lab table. Our kids don't need so much of that kind of prompting now; they know how much intrinsic fun science projects hold. But they still like to act as much like real scientists as they can. So I highly recommend pulling together items that make your children feel like real scientists to get things started.

Once you have those props and tools, it's also a good idea to make sure you have all the supplies you need to actually complete the project close at hand. I recommend reading or thinking through whatever experiment you're going to do thoroughly, making sure you understand the different steps and timing needed. Make sure to discuss these steps with your children as well. Of course you should also give some thought to any safety precautions you need to take. Sometimes those fancy safety goggles aren't just for dress-up! If an experiment calls for certain safety measures, make sure you understand them and discuss them with your children ahead of time. The particular measures you'll need to take will vary by experiment, but in general, I remind our children:

- I must be present to conduct most science experiments. At some point, some of the more exploratory projects become safe enough for them to handle on their own, but I want to make sure I'm around, just in case.

- Keep their fingers out of their eyes and away from their faces once we start an experiment. Getting something like baking soda in your eye is no fun.

- Wear safety gear when appropriate.

- No food or drink is allowed near the experiments.

- Slow down and wait for instructions.

SCIENCE LOVE!

Although I'm generally learning about many subjects as I go along with the kids, I actually have a science background. I studied ecology and biology in college in anticipation of going into environmental law, which I practiced after law school. So I can personally attest that having a foundation in science prepared me for all kinds of challenges in life, including being able to impart to my children just how gross it is to pick their noses.

Science is actually, well, a science. Measurements and the order of things matter, and children need to listen to instructions before they start making mixtures willy-nilly (unless, of course, that is exactly just what we're doing).

Once you're fairly confident that they understand how to be safe, I like to explain the scientific method in basic terms:

- Ask a question.

- Develop a hypothesis (a predictive answer to the question).

- Think of an experiment to test your hypothesis.

- Analyze the results of the experiment.

- Modify or repeat the experiment.

You can help show how to record and report this method as the children conduct their experiments. For example, in the basic coloring mixing project discussed in this section, you could narrate and write out the process:

(Question) *How do you make the color green?*
(Hypothesis) *I think green is made by mixing the primary colors blue and yellow.*
(Experiment) *I will mix equal parts blue water with equal parts yellow water.*
(Analysis) *Mixing those two colors made green.*
(Modification) *I will mix more blue water with less yellow water.*

If your children are starting to write, have them help write out these steps and record their observations. It doesn't need to be elaborate; even something as simple as marking boxes on a chart you've already drawn for them will work fine.

This all sounds a little serious, but it's all necessary for the next step—having fun! Once you have the basics covered, you'll need to pick a project. Not sure where to start? Don't worry—this chapter has some great ideas to get you started. If you have already started basic science experiments or are looking for something more advanced, amp up these experiments with more in-depth scientific explanations. Your local library's science section can be a great resource. We also frequently use the library to lay a knowledge foundation before conducting an experiment. And we often go back after we've wrapped up a project to follow up on additional questions that we raised. Science experiments are a great way to start teaching your children about research skills—especially with actual books instead of just relying on the Internet and Google. Depending on how old your kids are, you might even set up a brief lesson about research, including the authenticity, bias, and value of particular sources.

Science Project Ideas

In case you don't have a child who is interested in science for science's sake, I've found that the best way to approach science projects at home is to use one of two hooks: gross or fun. I know what you might be thinking: kids come up with so much gross stuff on their own that you might not want to encourage more—but they really do love gross science. For example, we have made many different kinds of slime, and although it may be messy and gross, kids unwittingly learn about polymers and have a great sensory experience. Even if you aren't looking to voluntarily bring projects like slime into your life, there are still plenty of other ideas. Read on for our favorite science projects, with options for extension activities. Get your little scientists started!

CHROMATOGRAPHY

Chromatography is a fancy name for a very simple concept: separating a mixture into its various chemical components. It's also a sure path to get your kids believing you can actually perform

magic. In our fun and simple version of chromatography, children will see the different pigments that actually make up one color of marker. This experiment works by placing chromatography paper with a line of marker into a solvent—in this case, water. As the water travels up the paper, it also dissolves the chemical mixture of the marker and pulls the chemicals up the paper. Some chemicals will dissolve well, and those will travel farther than the chemicals that do not— separating all the components across the paper. Children will learn basic scientific concepts, such as mixture and solvent, while doing what seems to be a little magic themselves.

Materials

- Chromatography paper
- Several brands of water-soluble black markers (not permanent!)
- A clear glass or jar
- A wooden craft stick or skewer
- Tape
- A pencil
- Water
- Vinegar or baby oil (optional)
- Coffee filters (optional)
- Colored markers (optional)

Directions

1. Talk to your kids about what a mixture is and how its components are often invisible to the naked eye.

2. Fill the glass or jar with a few inches of water.

3. Draw a line about a half-inch up from the bottom of the chromatography paper with the pencil. Label the top of the paper with the name of the marker brand. Draw a thick line of marker above the pencil line at the bottom of the paper. Repeat for each marker brand.

4. Put the stick across the top of the glass, and position the paper perpendicular to the stick. Tape the paper to the craft stick at a height so that only the bottom of the paper dips into the water. Be careful not to let the marker lines touch the water—submerse the paper below your pencil line only.

5. Watch the water travel up the paper, separating the mixture into its chemical components, which appear in different colors. Remove the strip of paper from the water when the marker reaches about one inch from the top so that you can look carefully at the separation (and even measure how far each color traveled). Cam also liked to let the experiment run until the mixture components all reached the very top of the paper and started to reform into a solid black color again. Even more magic!

Additional Options

- Compare the movement of the same marker using a different solvent. In addition to water, set up a glass containing vinegar or baby oil. (Safety caution: Breathing in baby oil can be fatal, so use it carefully!) Does the marker separate differently in the various solvents?

- Once you've tested all your markers, put them in a container and have each of the kids pick one out while keeping their eyes closed. Then run the experiment side by side, racing the markers against each other. You have an instant science competition! (Perform this competition with your child if he does not have any siblings or friends present.)

- If you don't want to invest in chromatography paper, try a similar experiment using flat-bottomed coffee filters. Draw a ring of marker midway between the center and edge of the flat part of the coffee filter, leaving enough blank space in the middle to dip in the water. (Remember—you don't want the marker to actually touch the water.) Fold the filter in half and then in half again so that it looks like a two-dimensional cone. With the waffled portion at the top, place the center tip of the coffee filter into the glass of water so just the blank filter space below the marker ring touches the water. Watch the filter wick the water up the cone, separating and spreading the marker's pigments. Try using other colors in addition to black to see if they are also a combination of pigments.

CLOUD VIEWING AND CLASSIFICATION

As soon as the weather gets warm, we try to spend lots and lots of time outdoors. Fresh air and exercise make everyone much happier, so we do all kinds of activities outside. Because I know that so much science gets done inside a lab when you're an older student, it's wonderful to show children how science happens outdoors. I imagine that many people don't think of weather as science, but it is a great way to introduce so many different scientific principles in a completely accessible way for children—because they can see it!

One of the best ways to get them started on learning about weather is to check out some clouds. I don't mean just looking for shapes in the clouds (although we do that too), but try to get the kids to help classify the types of clouds in the sky. First, you will want to explain the basic principles of precipitation and their roles in cloud formation. NASA offers a great explanation of the water cycle online (http://pmm.nasa.gov/education/water-cycle) that can help you.

I had seen several different kinds of cloud classification tools floating around online and knew that I could make my own, so I did. Our cloud viewer is a simple handheld viewfinder

that allows children to compare what they spot in the sky with photos of the following cloud types: altocumulus, altostratus, cirrocumulus, cirrostratus, cirrus, cumulonimbus, cumulus, nimbostratus, stratocumulus, and stratus. You can download the viewer for free from our blog (search for "cloud viewer" and click on the link in the text for the template). NASA's website also provides a great video tutorial you can use to help explain the various cloud types to your children (http://science-edu.larc.nasa.gov/SCOOL/tutorial/clouds/newusers-CT.html).

Our kids quickly fell in love with the concept and continued thereafter to categorize whatever clouds we spotted in the sky. And they still get a big kick out of me pretending that I don't know the cloud types. I think part of it is that they like teaching me, but most of it is probably them just embracing our family's joy in giving each other a good-natured hard time.

Materials

- A Not-So-SAHM cloud classification tool

- A comfy blanket

- Some good clouds

Directions

1. Discuss ahead of time the different types of clouds and how each kind is formed. Lie down, and hold up the cloud classification tool to the sky.

2. Have your kids pick which picture on the tool matches a particular cloud. You can help correct them if they get it wrong, but stay positive and show them why you might pick a different type of cloud.

3. Follow up at home with any weather-related questions.

- If you are finding only one type of cloud, you can still add variety to the activity. Once you're done classifying the clouds, turn the activity back into an exciting game of looking for shapes. Help your kids tell a story with the shapes they're seeing in the sky (sort of like the stories attached to constellations)—a dragon chasing an airplane, a bunny riding waves, and so on.

- Turn your classifications into an art project! Use cotton balls to practice making different types of clouds by scrunching and stretching the cotton balls into the correct shapes and gluing them on paper. For really young children, outline a shape on a page (like a bunny, for example) and let them glue cotton balls to it—making a cloud animal.

- Use the classification project as a springboard to other weather-related science experiments (such as the mason-jar science experiments later in this chapter).

COLOR MIXING

This is a classic project for children. It's part science and part art, and it includes many activities young kids enjoy, especially making messes. You can give children a few cups of water and see how much time they can spend just pouring the water from one cup to another. (In the winter, I like to fill up the bathtub and let them do just that—for hours.) If you add in some fun colors, you can really bump up your game. Although this might seem like an activity for the youngest ones, you can really adapt this to suit any child's age and level of science aptitude with the addition

of a few simple pieces of equipment. I like it best for teaching the fundamentals of the scientific method (as explained in the previous section, Preparing for Science Experiments), introducing science and math concepts (such as *more than* and *less than*), and teaching kids how to use basic science equipment (test tubes, beakers, and pipettes).

Materials

- Food coloring or color tablets
- Water
- Clear cups, test tubes, beakers, or graduated cylinders large enough to hold a good amount of liquid
- Paper and pencil
- Plastic pipettes (optional, but these give children more control over the amount of liquid they are mixing together)
- A spill tray (optional, but this helps avoid having to stop and clean up in the middle of the project)
- Oil and syrup (optional)
- Water beads (optional)

Directions

1. Fill three cups or graduated cylinders with water. Plastic cups work well for preschoolers, but you can use a container with marked measurements for older children.
2. Have the children add red, yellow, and blue colors, respectively (using either food coloring or color tablets).
3. Help your kids walk through the first three steps of the scientific method, and record their hypothesis and planned experiment using paper and pencil. For example, one dropper of blue + one dropper of yellow = ?
4. Have the children pour the desired colors together in a separate container. (If they have the fine motor skills to squeeze plastic pipettes, they can use these tools to mix the colors.)
5. Record the result, and try again!

Additional Options

- Once your child has figured out what two primary colors to mix to achieve a particular secondary color, try to vary the amounts of those two primary colors to create different shades of the same secondary color. Our science club of four- and five-year-olds loved doing this because they already knew which secondary colors would come from mixing certain primaries. Cameron made about a million different shades of purple.

- Instead of using water, pick a few liquids of varying densities (oil, syrup, and water) and color them with the three primary colors. Pour them into a tall, clear container, and see how the liquids separate and change colors as they mix. If you color the liquids with careful consideration of their density, you can make a rainbow!

- Soak clear, water-soluble beads or crystals in containers of water colored in two different primary colors. Layer two colors of beads or crystals together in a test tube, and hold that up to a light. See if the overlapping edge creates a secondary color.

FUN WITH DRY ICE

Experimenting with dry ice can be tricky; children really need to understand the safety issues involved with using this frozen form of carbon dioxide. Dry ice requires adult supervision and is not safe to touch or swallow. As the dry ice turns into gas, you do not want to breathe in much of it. Dry ice can burn skin easily upon direct contact. Also, it is not always the easiest material to find. But when used under adult supervision, basic experiments with dry ice earn big oohs and aahs. These types of experiments can spike children's interest in science really quickly. If you have very young children, however, I'd make sure they are somewhere safe where they can watch but not touch. Otherwise, it's just too tempting. The National Weather Service has a good explanation of the safety issues on its website (http://www.wrh.noaa.gov/vef/kids/dryice.php).

Materials

- Small pieces of dry ice
- Insulated gloves
- Tongs
- A glass or plastic container
- Warm water
- A plate (optional)
- Fabric strips (optional)
- Dishwashing liquid (optional)
- Food coloring (optional)

OUR PLANS DRIED UP!

We first tried this experiment with dry ice that came with a delivery from our grocery store. Our groceries were delivered one morning, and the idea of making clouds popped into my head. But we didn't have enough time to do it before our day got started. I told our kids my idea, and we excitedly decided to wait until later in the day to try it. I closed the box up tight (it was still ventilated), full of additional ice packs, and we set off on our day. We returned home later and opened the box, only to find that the dry ice had disappeared! Whoops! I hadn't really thought it through, and of course the dry ice had evaporated when left in the box. So we had done an unplanned science experiment before we'd even had a chance to make clouds! But the kids were hooked. I planned better the next time, and we did the experiment first thing upon grocery delivery, and at night with flashlights—spooky!

Directions

1. Make sure you are working in a well-ventilated area. We like to try this experiment outside.

2. Fill a container about halfway with warm water (cold water will not work as well).

3. With everyone wearing gloves and using tongs, have the kids help you place a piece of dry ice into the water.

4. Watch as the dry ice turns into carbon dioxide gas and water vapor, creating clouds that will bubble out over the top of the container and down onto the surrounding surface. The clouds are safe to touch briefly, but make sure they do not touch the dry ice directly!

5. As the dry ice cools the water, add more warm water to continue the cloud effect.

Additional Options

- After you've done the basic dry ice experiment above, ask your kids what they think will happen if you leave a piece of dry ice out on a plate. Most kids know that ice melts when left sitting out, so chances are that is what they will hypothesize. Leave it for a few hours and check on it periodically. They will be amazed to see that it basically disappears! Then you have a mystery to solve.

- Help your little artists get interested in science by adding a few squirts of dishwashing liquid into a bowl of colored water. Then add a piece of dry ice and watch the carbon dioxide and soap combine and bubble out over the top. Gently press a piece of paper to the top of the bubbles to make a bubble print! Experiment by adding additional colors.

- Catch that gas in a bubble! Place a piece of dry ice in a bowl with a rounded edge and add water, filling up the bowl about halfway. Pour a few squirts of dishwashing liquid into a cup of water and mix well. Soak a long strip of fabric (a piece of a dish towel or a shoelace will work) in the soapy mixture. Pull the fabric strip out of the soap and coat the rounded edge of the bowl with the soapy fabric. Then stretch the fabric horizontally with two hands and pull it across the top of the bowl until you see a bubble starting to form!

FAKE SNOW

Unlike many of the other science experiments included in this book, making fake snow requires the purchase of a special compound: sodium polyacrylate, which is a polymer that absorbs water and expands to make a material resembling snow. Although this project draws children in with its magic-like appeal, it also helps teach them the basics of polymers, in addition to important scientific concepts (such as cause-and-effect measurements, physical reactions, and absorption and osmosis). Have you ever wondered how those disposable

diapers work? This is how. But I recommend testing out sodium polyacrylate's absorption properties with fake snow instead of watching an over-wet diaper grow.

Materials

- Sodium polyacrylate (search for it or "snow polymer" online)
- Plastic pipettes or droppers
- Several dishes
- Water
- Salt (optional)
- Liquid watercolors (optional)
- Other accessories (optional)

Directions

1. Pour a small amount of sodium polyacrylate into a dish.
2. Using a plastic pipette, slowly drop water onto the material.
3. Watch the polymer seem to explode as it absorbs water.
4. Experiment by adding additional polymer or water to reach the desired amount and consistency of snow.
5. Let children dig their hands in and play with the fake snow.

Additional Options

- Adding water to the polymer illustrates the basic process of osmosis: the water travels from an area of dilute solution outside the polymer into the polymer's more highly concentrated solution. Once the polymer has absorbed the water, try reversing that process by adding salt to the mixture, which creates a more highly concentrated solution on the outside of the polymer. You will then see the water flow back out, and you'll get mush instead of snow.
- For those children who are more artistically inclined, turn the experiment into an art project. We like to add liquid watercolors to polymer snow play and have an art and story-playing session. Kane likes to make igloos and forts, and wage war between the different colors of snow he makes. Cam copies

STORY PLAYING

All kinds of activities lend themselves to what I call *story playing*, which is sort of akin to make-believe, but involves the kids playing out a particular story. Sometimes they like to play out a storyline from a book we're reading, sometimes they make up the story ahead of time, and sometimes we just improvise.

one of our favorite multicolored treats from Northern Michigan and makes us pretend Superman ice cream. (Caution—no eating allowed!)

- Add fun accessories to reuse your experiment material for sensory play. Use small molds (such as cupcake molds), large spoons or ice cream scoopers, or small toys. See if the children can build shapes using the material or pretend that it is something else entirely (sand to make pyramids, ice cream for an ice cream shop, and so on).

LAVA LAMPS

This project definitely falls under the cool category, because you can really sneak some science in without the kids noticing much. If they are more advanced in science at this point, you can adapt the experiment up to their knowledge level. This is essentially an experiment about molecular polarity and density using water and oil. Water molecules like to stick together. Oil molecules like to stick together as well. But the two kinds of molecules don't like to stick to each other. In addition, this experiment illustrates density in several ways:

- Oil is less dense than water, so you'll see it float on top.

- Carbon dioxide is lighter than water, so you'll see the gas created by dissolved seltzer tablets rise to the top.

- The gas brings a bit of colored water up with it, which gets released when the air bubble pops and the heavier water sinks back down through the oil.

You could just pour some oil and water together in a glass to get the gist of these scientific principles, but this is so much more fun!

Materials

- A tall bottle

- Cooking oil (enough to fill up 3/4 of the bottle)

- Water

- Food coloring

- Fizzy antacid tablets (such as Alka-Seltzer)

- Submersible light or flashlight

- Glitter (optional)

- Salt (optional)

Directions

1. Let the kids fill three-fourths of the bottle with cooking oil.

2. They can fill the remainder with water, but not quite all the way to the top. You'll need some room for bubbling.

3. Have the kids add a few drops of food coloring.

4. Leaving the top of the bottle off, let the kids break up the fizzy tablet and drop it in a bit at a time. Watch what happens to the gas bubbles created and observe the rising droplets of colored water.

5. Add a submersible light, which will float on top and light downward, or shine a flashlight up from the outside bottom for a more realistic lava lamp effect.

Additional Options

- Do you have a child who likes to sparkle? Add a healthy dose of glitter to the water first and see what happens when you add the fizzy tablet.

- Try creating a reverse lava lamp effect by sprinkling a little bit of salt onto the top of the oil (after all your fizzy tablets have fizzled out). The salt is heavier than water, so when you sprinkle it on the oil, it will sink through the mixture and carry a bit of oil with it down through the water. When the salt dissolves in the water, it releases the oil, which will then float back up to the top of the water.

- Spend some more time observing density. When the fizzy tablet is gone, replace the bottle top and tip the bottle back and forth. Shake it in different directions. Help the kids make observations about what is happening.

Mason-Jar Science

Mason-jar science experiments are great projects to do on short notice because many of them use items that you're likely to already have at home. Plus because they are mostly contained in a jar, they are not as messy as other experiments. And—always important to me—you can do a wide range of projects to suit different children's personalities. Our three favorite mason-jar science experiments are the Bouncy Egg, Make It Rain, and Fireworks in a Jar. Together, the experiments expose children to a variety of scientific principles and disciplines, including chemistry, atmospheric science, and another look at density. When we first did these projects, Kane was fascinated by the gross bouncy egg but seemed entirely unimpressed with making it rain inside of a jar. Cameron, on the other hand, wanted nothing to do with the disgusting egg but was fascinated that she was "controlling the weather." If you get everything set up well, you can work with your kids' different personalities to do some of these projects at the same time—focusing on their individual interests.

THE BOUNCY EGG

The point of this cool (and somewhat gross) experiment is to illustrate the chemical reaction of decalcification—where the acidic vinegar reacts with the calcium carbonate in the egg shell, making it softer, weaker, and then eventually completely dissolving it. And further, it then continues to denature the protein in the egg, turning the outer portion rubbery. The chemical reaction gives off carbon dioxide, which you can see in the form of bubbles. It also illustrates the concept of osmosis by showing how the water in the vinegar moves through the semipermeable membrane of the egg (once the shell is dissolved) from an area of higher water concentration outside the egg to an area of lower water concentration inside the egg. As a result, the egg will grow in size. This provides so many different science lessons in just one experiment! Also it's just really cool to bounce a raw egg. But make sure to have your child wear safety goggles—we didn't the first time and Kane unfortunately got an eye full of vinegar-soaked egg. It was not pretty. This experiment also requires patience and forty-eight hours to complete.

Materials

- A glass mason jar
- A raw egg (If possible, use a brown-shelled egg—it's easier to observe in the experiment.)
- Vinegar
- Safety goggles

- Food coloring (optional)

- Corn syrup (optional)

- Water (optional)

Directions

1. Have your child carefully place the egg in the mason jar and fill the jar with vinegar.

2. Ask children to record their observations of what's happening in the jar several hours apart.

3. After twenty-four hours, very carefully remove the egg and change the vinegar. (It will be pretty dirty already from the reaction.) Let the kids gently explore the egg and make any additional observations. Place the egg back in the new vinegar.

4. After forty-eight hours, children can remove the egg from the jar. Hold it up to the light to get a good look at the reaction that has occurred.

5. Wearing safety goggles, the children can gently bounce the egg a short distance from a surface. If you like, they can increase the bouncing distance until the egg breaks!

Additional Options

- Conduct an additional experiment with the vinegar-soaked egg before you bounce it. Try placing it in a jar of water mixed with food coloring. Now that the eggshell has been dissolved, more water will be able to enter through the semipermeable membrane, causing the egg to increase in size again. And you'll be able to see the colored water moving into the egg.

- If you want to make the egg shrink in size, place the vinegar-soaked egg in corn syrup. You now have a higher concentration of water inside the egg than outside. So water will leave the egg and cause it to shrink.

- After your children have the basics of observation down, try the experiment again. Start a new egg in vinegar, but also set up a second mason jar with an additional raw egg in water so they can compare the two experiments. After forty-eight hours is up, find a place where you can contain the mess and bounce both eggs. Our kids think it's hysterical to drop an egg they know will splatter!

MAKE IT RAIN

This experiment doesn't have as big of a wow factor as some of the others, but if you have a child who's interested in weather or who likes to ask a lot of *why* questions, this just might be the perfect experiment. On any given day, Cameron asks an endless number of questions about

how and why certain things work. I was happy to be able to answer at least one of them with this easy project. Kane, on the other hand, found this less than spectacular, so he had to infuse a little magic in; he claimed to be able to make accurate observations of what was happening because he could read my mind. (I think I'd approach this one with him a little differently next time—see the Additional Options section.)

In simple terms, this experiment illustrates that when warmer, moist air meets colder air, the moisture in the warm air condenses and falls out. When you add hot water to the mason jar and cap it, some of the water evaporates into the air inside. When that air meets the cold plate at the top, the water droplets in the air condense and fall down the side of the jar like rain. It's an easy project with very little wait time!

Materials

- A glass mason jar (with the metal top)
- A small plate
- Hot water
- Ice cubes

- A weather-related book (optional)

- A cup (optional)

- Room-temperature water (optional)

- Shaving cream (optional)

- Food coloring (optional)

- A pipette or dropper (optional)

Directions

1. Fill the mason jar three-fourths of the way with hot water and screw the metal lid on. Cover the lid with the plate and let it sit for a few minutes while the water warms up the air inside.

2. Have the children place ice cubes onto the plate.

3. Watch as the cold plate cools the air inside the jar, making condensation run down the sides of the jar.

Additional Options

- If you have a child who loves to look for rational explanations of why the world works as it does, this is a great project. Of course, that's exactly what science involves. If you have a child who prefers fantastical reasons, loop him in to learning science through that interest. For example, Kane is obsessed with all things Greek mythology. He particularly

loves Zeus, the god of the sky and thunder. So I think it would be really fun to work this experiment into a story-playing session and let Kane pretend he's Zeus, making it rain. Alternatively, you could pick a favorite book that is also weather related (such as *Cloudy with a Chance of Meatballs*) and tie the experiment in to that story. The children will learn the science without realizing it.

- Take the experiment a bit further to show how rain comes from clouds, which are formed from condensed water. When those condensed water droplets become too heavy, rain falls from the clouds. Get a cup of water and mix in blue food coloring. Instead of placing the lid and a plate of ice on the top of your mason jar, make a sort of cloud out of shaving cream on top of a jar completely filled with room-temperature water. Using a pipette, drop colored water into the shaving cream cloud. When it gets too full, the colored water will drop down into the jar and you'll see the rain coming through. This is a great way to get an artistic child interested in science as well.

- Look for other examples of condensation (such as iced water in a drinking glass or a cold can left sitting out) and discuss how similar principles of condensation apply.

FIREWORKS IN A JAR

This experiment is another way to show kids how the concept of density works. Plus it is a great activity for children who love art. Similar to the homemade lava lamps, the science behind this display of art comes from the reaction between oil and water. When you gently mix food coloring into oil, the color becomes suspended in the mixture. It doesn't dissolve without vigorous mixing. When you add the oil mixture to water, however, the food coloring mixes immediately with the water, dropping out of the oil and making little explosions of color. This is because food coloring is hydrophilic (it likes water), whereas oil is hydrophobic (it does not like water). Our kids did this experiment over and over again, amazed each time at the different displays of color created.

Materials

- A glass mason jar
- A shallow plate
- Warm water
- Cooking oil
- Gel food colors
- A toothpick (optional)
- A piece of white paper (optional)
- A small shallow container (optional)

Carefully swirl the colors around in the water—it won't mix with the oil, so it will make pretty designs.

Directions

1. Fill the mason jar three-fourths of the way with warm water.

2. Let the children pour three tablespoons of oil onto the shallow plate, and then carefully drop food coloring onto the oil.

3. They can mix the oil and food coloring gently with a fork, making sure the food coloring stays in droplet form. The gel food coloring works much better than liquid for this reason.

4. As children pour the oil and food coloring into the water, they can watch the visual explosion of colors—like fireworks!

Additional Options

- Turn the experiment into an art project. Make extra of the oil and food coloring mixture, but this time mix it really, really well. (Mix one color at a time with oil to get several different colors.) Fill a shallow container halfway with water. Add the colored oil. Using a toothpick, carefully swirl the colors around in the water—it won't mix with the oil, so it will make pretty designs. Place a piece of white paper on top of the container and lift. The water will pick up the colored oil design and create marbled art! (See our blog and search for "marbling" to find additional marbling art projects.)

- Combine this experiment with the previous color mixing experiment. Once your kids get a good handle on how the experiment works, have them predict how they can make a new color from adding different primary-colored oils.

- After you've had your fill of visual fireworks, pour the oil and water mixture into a plastic container, add a bit of extra oil, and then let the whole mixture separate into distinct layers. Have your child place it in the freezer and then wait a few hours. What happens? The water expands as it freezes, making it less dense than the oil. The kids will be surprised to see that the frozen water is now on top of the oil!

SENSORY PROJECTS

I hope the previous chapter showed you that even if you do not consider yourself a science nerd (as I consider myself), you can find lots of easy ways to get kids into science so they enjoy it. However, if you're looking for some activities that kids view as just a really good time, then you are in the right section. Very simply put, sensory projects are anything that stimulates your kids' senses, including sight, smell, taste, touch, and hearing. You can find information on a myriad of growth and developmental benefits from sensory play, including developing motor skills, improving problem solving, and learning language. But we've always done these types of projects because they are an enjoyable way to explore! And that's exactly how kids look at them as well.

Now this is absolutely the section for super-fun projects, but I will warn you that sensory exploration is messy (even by my standards). I generally look for sensory projects that have a strong positive correlation between

the time spent playing and the time spent cleaning up, so the mess is worth it. Where possible, I do try to contain the mess. But even considering the tendency toward mayhem, I'd still encourage you to try some of these sensory projects with your kids. I think once you see just how much they enjoy these activities, you'll relax a little and go with the flow. However, I should note—especially because I have no background or training in areas such as occupational therapy or neuroscience—that there are some children who cannot stand these types of activities. So be sensitive to that possibility, and make sure you're not pushing just for the sake of the project. If the kids are not enjoying it at all, reevaluate whether these kinds of projects are the right fit for them or if you might need some assistance in figuring out the best way to engage their senses.

Preparing for Sensory Projects

By now, you probably have a good sense that these projects take a little bit of planning to pull together. But if you involve the kids in the prep and cleanup of the project, you'll get an even better experience out of it. Once you pick a project, spend some time thinking about how you want to contain the mess. I like to use a spill tray, cover a table with a drop cloth, use a metal or plastic tub or bin, or even put the kids right in the bathtub to start.

For the most part, I involve our kids in making the sensory product itself. If you have younger kids, I suggest premeasuring ingredients and handling any necessary real cooking by yourself. But I try to let our kids do as much of the making as I think they can safely handle. It makes the activity more fun, introduces and reinforces scientific concepts, and extends the activity time too. If you add in prep work to the play time and tack on baths at the end, you can easily have one project take up an entire afternoon—which, I'm sure you can imagine, is so much better than spending an hour setting up a project, having the kids play with it for five minutes, and then doing an hour of cleanup by yourself.

Sensory Project Ideas

For almost all of our kids' young lives, we lived in the middle of the city with no yard. So water play for us has always meant bathtub or water table time. If you're lucky enough to have outdoor space, pretty much all of these activities can be done outside, which will certainly cut down on the cleanup. But if you don't or there's bad weather, rest assured that you can still do water play indoors and with very little space. We have an actual water table designed for kids, but a plain old plastic tub or bin will work just as well. These activities always seem to keep my children occupied for serious amounts of time, but they involve very little setup and—especially when done in the bathtub—are easy to clean up. I'm including our basic favorites, but you can do so many variations depending on your child's interest and your tolerance for mess.

SHAVING-CREAM TUB PAINT

Every time our kids shower in our bathroom, they go nuts with the shaving cream. They turn it into "cleaning soap" and smear it all over the glass; they grow pretend shaving-cream beards; they write messages; they create a car wash. And they just generally use up all of our good bath product. So I knew they would love some of their own! No need to buy the expensive stuff—get whatever is on sale and will make a nice, big foam.

Materials

- Small plastic cups
- Several cans of shaving cream
- Washable liquid watercolors, tempera paint, or fingerpaints (Washable is key to avoid staining your tub.)
- Paintbrushes or sponges
- Metallic paint or glitter (optional)
- A plastic tub or water table (optional)
- An acrylic easel (optional)

Directions

1. Fill each plastic cup with shaving cream.

2. Add in a few drops of paint and mix well.

3. Put your kids in the bathtub or shower and let them go to town! They can paint the tub, the walls, or themselves. When they're done, have them help wash it all off and take a bath!

Additional Options

- For kids who love sparkle, add metallic paint or glitter to the mix.

- If you want to try this outdoors (either in a water table or a plastic tub), consider adding an acrylic easel for painting. (You can see an example on our blog.) Bump up the play time by incorporating the tub paint into a themed bath.

GLOW-IN-THE-DARK TUB PAINTING

This one actually needs to be done indoors and in a bathtub—even I have limits to my tolerance for mess! But if you take a little time to get it set up and suspend your urge to immediately wipe paint off of your tile, your children will have a great time. There is something special about adding in the sensory experience of fluorescence that makes children love this project. And I do think that kids are psyched when they get to do a messy activity that makes them feel they're coloring outside of the lines, so to speak. This project is basically you saying to your kids: "Yes! Go ahead and paint all over the bathroom tile and yourself!" So take a deep breath, remember it will all wash away, and let them play!

Materials

- Small plastic cups or a painting tray
- Washable fluorescent paint
- A black lightbulb
- Tape
- Paintbrushes or sponges
- Large pieces of poster board or heavy-weight paper (optional)
- Music (optional)
- Other fluorescent items (optional)

Directions

1. Replace a bathroom lightbulb with a black light.
2. If you're using poster board or paper, tape it up to the walls of your bathtub as high as you think the kids will reach. It's not necessary, though. You can also let your kids just paint right on the bathroom tile if you're comfortable with that. But if you don't want to have to wash the walls or are interested in keeping the art your kids make during the project, then you will want to take this extra step.
3. Fill plastic cups or the tray with several different colors of fluorescent paint. Washable paint is key to avoid staining your tub.
4. Add the paintbrushes and sponges.
5. Turn off all the lights in the bathroom and turn on the black light.
6. Hand over the paints and materials and let them get creative!
7. When they're done, turn off and remove the black light, and let them clean themselves in the bath.

Additional Options

- Play music and add a few other items that fluoresce (such as glow-in-the-dark rubber duckies or paintbrushes taped to glow sticks) to make this a real party!
- Everyday games are so much more entertaining when done with fluorescent paint. Help

your kids draw a tic-tac-toe board on the wall to play with paintbrushes. Or try a game where you draw clues to help others guess a word or phrase.

- If you hung poster board or paper, save the art the kids made and have them help you turn it into colorful decorations such as a garland. They'll love to look at it and remember the fun project.

THEMED WATER PLAY

As you might have gleaned from the book so far, my kids love bath time. They spend hours in the shower and bathtub, playing, listening to audiobooks, creating art, and more. But I could not believe how much more time they spend in there with a little bit of extra setup from me. It started with a random frantic idea on a long, cold winter day. I decided to throw them a tropical bathtub party just to get them to stop picking at each other, but now I do themed water play regularly (and often less elaborately) just to make some fun. When it's warm out, I'll set up our water table in the same way, so they can play outside. In addition to stretching out bath time, I love that themed water play can easily be done with so many random objects you have in your home. Once you start looking, you'll be amazed at what you can pull together. You can either start with an idea (such as a holiday) and then look around your home for things to use, or look first and see what makes sense (such as a rainbow-themed water table with a variety of colored objects).

Materials

- A bathtub, bin, or water table

- Water

- An assortment of items for your theme, such as toys, recycled containers, and items for building (For our Valentine's Day bath, I collected all the red and pink toys I could find in our home that I was comfortable letting get wet.)

- Decorations, such as food coloring to color the water, streamers to hang around the bathtub, or even glitter

- One or two sensory items—shaving cream for bathtub play, sand for the water table, or ice cubes for either one

Directions

1. Get your bath or table all set up. Add the water, color it, hang any decorations, and set out the items you've gathered.

2. Call the kids, and let them explore!

3. When they're done, enlist their help in cleanup, which is easier if they are already in the bathtub.

Additional Options

- If the weather is warm, expand these themed play ideas to the neighborhood with a large, blow-up kiddie pool.

- Children who are fascinated with how things work tend to enjoy playing with man-made manipulations of water. Turn this play into engineering fun by adding materials to help the kids make dams, diversions, and more with the water in a shallow water table.

- If you're using a water table, look for opportunities to loop science into this activity. Add dirt, sand, and plants (real or fake) to help make a model and show older children the basics of the hydrological cycle. Add ice, and talk about glacial science. Make a sandy beach, and talk about waves. The options to include science are really endless.

CLOUD DOUGH

You won't find me hopping into the bathtub to make fluorescent paintings, but if we are making cloud dough, chances are that I'll be spending the afternoon with the kids playing with this

fabulous material. It's an incredibly cool tactile experience that works well for children of any age. However, make sure they don't put it anywhere near their mouths! You can keep this project really simple and present the cloud dough all on its own, or you can add a variety of tools to amp up the play a bit. Play around with the ratio of the two ingredients until you get the desired consistency. Safety caution: Breathing in baby oil can be fatal, so keep it out of reach of the children, and don't breathe it in yourself!

Materials

- A deep bin or tub
- Flour
- Baby oil
- Materials to use as molds (optional)
- Toys for pretend fossils (optional)

Directions

1. Using your hands, mix together flour and baby oil in a ratio of roughly 8:1. You can fiddle with it to get the exact consistency you like, but generally we do 4 cups of flour to 1/2 cup baby oil. Remember, a little baby oil goes a long way, so start out with a small amount of it.

2. Let your kids explore and play with the dough in creative ways!

Additional Options

- Add anything that will work as a small mold (silicone muffin cups or ice cube trays work awesomely) and let the kids mold shapes out of the dough. They can use them to make sculptures or build larger objects.

- Use the dough as a flexible material to make fossils. Press toy dinosaur tracks into the dough, or make a ball of cloud dough around a small toy and excavate it.

HEAD IN THE CLOUDS

The first time we made cloud dough, I kept it pretty simple and let the kids experience the texture on its own for a while. Now that they are cloud dough pros, they ask for toys to turn the dough into some kind of background for whatever story they are cooking up. The dough becomes castle walls, hills, sand dunes, and on and on.

- When they've had their fill of free play, use the cloud dough to help the kids learn a bit about science. Remind them about the types of clouds you discussed during the Cloud Viewing and Classification activity (in chapter 2), and help your kids shape the cloud dough into various types of clouds.

FROZEN SHAVING CREAM

I've called this fabulous sensory material *frozen playdough* before, but that term can be confusing. So let's call it what it is: *frozen shaving cream*. Freezing this everyday substance makes a moldable material that is unlike any other we've used. In the winter, we like to pretend it's snow; in the warmer months, we tend to pretend it's a frozen treat. Just make sure the children know not to eat the colorful frozen substance! The kids love it any time of year and will spend plenty of time playing with it. But whatever they pretend it is, our kids' entrepreneurial tendencies kick in and they will try to sell whatever they are making to anyone who will listen. And if there is anyone who can sell pretend ice in the middle of winter, it's those two.

Materials

- Shaving cream
- Plastic containers
- Washable liquid tempera paint
- A large bowl
- A mixing spoon
- A freezer
- Fun accessories

- Baking extracts (optional)

- Easel (optional)

- Paintbrushes (optional)

- Ice cube trays (optional)

- Sensory bin (optional)

Note: Do not use liquid watercolors or food coloring; they'll melt the shaving cream. Gel food colors work but are not washable.

Directions

1. Mix shaving cream and a few squirts of tempera paint in the large bowl. Add more color or cream until you get the desired color. If you add too much color and the cream starts to deflate, just mix in some more shaving cream. You're looking to keep the colored shaving cream roughly the same consistency as when it comes out of the can.

2. Scoop the mixture into a plastic container and then repeat for each color. Place all containers in the freezer for a few hours.

3. Once the shaving cream has set nicely, remove from the freezer and let the kids go to town playing with it.

Additional Options

- If the smell of shaving cream is not for you, consider adding in baking extracts (such as peppermint, vanilla, almond, and so on) prior to freezing. Just be careful not to add so much that the cream turns to liquid before making it into the freezer. Remember, too, that the attractive smell can make it more tempting for kids to taste the off-limits chemical substance—so emphasize safety!

FROZEN DELIGHTS

We made several batches of colored shaving cream recently, and I froze it into recycled gelato containers. (Of course, I gave the kids a stern warning: "No licking or eating!") The kids decided to set up a gelato bar named La Dolce Vita, and Cami proceeded to speak only in "Italian" for the rest of the afternoon. I understood her pointed gestures and shoving "gelato" under my face better than I would actual Italian, so it worked out just fine.

- Turn the sensory experience into art. Set up an easel outdoors, and let the children use their hands or paintbrushes to paint with the frozen foam.

- Stuck indoors in the winter? Freeze the shaving cream in ice cube containers, and have your kids build igloos in a sensory bin.

LIGHT BOXES

Light boxes are one of those sensory tools that look really cool, but their utility is not entirely clear until you start exploring with one. When I first saw these circulating online, I wasn't sure what we would actually use them for, but I knew that I wanted them. And then we really started using ours for all kinds of interesting sensory explorations. Like many sensory projects, the draw for kids isn't necessarily obvious, but they will use them for hours upon hours of play. You can buy fancy, expensive light trays and boxes, but I highly recommend making this easy, do-it-yourself one first. We have stuck with our original light boxes, and they have worked excellently. Sometimes I plan a more focused project with them (such as exploring X-rays together), and then at other times I just set them up with some interesting objects. They come in handy on days when the weather is bad and I'm looking for anything different to break up the day.

Materials

- A frosted plastic container with lid (Pick any size you like, but I prefer one that has a big enough lid surface to hold several objects.)

- White primer spray and silver spray paint

- A pluggable light source that will fit fully into the container with the lid closed, with the exception of the cord (You can try using a battery-operated light source to avoid dealing with the cord, but in my experience, those don't provide enough light.)

- A variety of materials that are fun to explore with light (for example, brightly colored plastic or glass cups, beads, and building materials)

- A small, clear-plastic storage tray or container a bit smaller than the size of the light box lid, so the tray can sit on top and hold the play materials (optional, but it makes cleanup easier)

Directions

1. Spray the inside of the bottom only of your plastic container with white primer spray, and let dry completely.

2. Spray the inside of the bottom only of the plastic container with several coats of silver spray paint, allowing each layer to dry completely in between.

3. Assemble your light source and place it in the bottom of the dry container. To keep it simple and avoid drilling any holes in the container, we let the cord trail over the top rim of the container and loosely place the lid on top.

4. Plug in the light.

5. Place your tray on top with assorted materials for exploration.

6. Let the kids play!

Additional Options

- Go pure sensory by adding multicolored water beads to the top of the light box. Use a variety of tools (such as chopsticks, spoons, or straws) to sort the beads by color, make patterns, or simply squish them (see the Water Beads section for a full discussion).

- Turn the exploration into a science lesson by adding any kind of X-ray films to the top of the light boxes. Label human bones, discover fossils, and look for patterns. The options are endless.

- Set up an exciting snack time by adding translucent squares of gelatin to the clean top. After your kids wash their hands, they can make edible sculptures and explore the fun, squishy material.

PLAYDOUGH

I vividly remember making homemade playdough with my mother—the warm, soft dough, and the incredibly salty taste! We must have made it around Halloween, because I remember making a big, orange batch of it. I can still see it sitting in the brown mixing bowl in our kitchen (the same bowl into which we were required to collectively put our Halloween candy, much to all four kids' dismay). Given this fond memory, playdough was one of the very first sensory projects I did with my own kids. No matter what age they are, it has always been one of their favorite things to make and play with. It's such a great, open-ended sensory medium that

allows them to use their imaginations while strengthening motor skills and even learning a little about science and cooking.

Over the years, we've made all sorts of playdough and tested out all kinds of recipes, and even though we tweak it now and then, we generally find ourselves starting back with the same basic recipe. We included several of our winning playdough activities in the Additional Options section, but feel free to head over to our blog for more playdough madness. Just use your own imagination to add to these starting points and adapt the activity to whatever interests you and your kids most.

Materials

- 4 cups flour
- 4 cups water
- 1 cup salt
- 2 tablespoons cooking oil
- 4 teaspoons cream of tartar
- A smidge of baby oil
- Food coloring
- Markers and stamps (optional)
- Assorted food items, craft supplies, and tools (optional)

GLUTEN-FREE PLAYDOUGH

If you would like to make gluten-free playdough, substitute masa corn flour for regular flour. You'll need about 1 additional cup of the masa corn flour (for a total of 5 cups) to fold in at the end of cooking to help reduce stickiness.

Directions

1. Combine flour, water, salt, cooking oil, and cream of tartar in a large pot. Cook over medium heat, stirring constantly until most of the moisture is absorbed. Depending on your children's ages and your comfort with them cooking safely, you will probably want to handle the cooking part yourself.

2. Place the cooked batch onto wax paper to let it cool a bit. While the dough is still warm to the touch, add baby oil and work it in. (Careful with the baby oil—it can be fatal if inhaled!)

3. Divide the batch into smaller portions, add a bit of food coloring to each, and let the kids mix and fold the color in. It can take a bit of time, so if you're looking for a quicker way to do this, you can add the food coloring to the water before you combine the ingredients in the first step. You will get only one color of playdough per batch that way, though.

Additional Options

- Leave out the food coloring and cook up a batch of plain playdough. Once it cools, give your kids old markers or stamps and let them color the dough themselves! The first time we did this, Kane rolled out the playdough and colored it into a three-dimensional landscape for his pirate toys, and made water, waves, an island, and more. Cam added

polka dots to hers and then rolled it around until it was tie-dyed. Kids can come up with endless creative options!

- Mix in food items to the basic recipe for some fun cooking play. Try adding one-third cup of cocoa powder to get a really yummy-scented chocolate playdough. Add in some baking tools and make your own dessert bakery with it. Do you have sushi fans in your house? Add uncooked sushi rice to the cooked playdough for an interesting extrasensory experience. Some seaweed sheets and sushi accessories take it a step further as they make awesome-looking rolls. However, if you use any food items, make sure you supply real food snacks to satisfy the kids' appetites and keep them from tasting the playdough.

- Add any kind of scent (baking extracts, spices, or essential oils work well) to the cooked dough to add even more to the sensory experience. We love to add scents such as vanilla or peppermint. And especially in the winter, essential oils can have great aromatherapy effects. Check a reliable source first, however, as some oils are not safe for children.

- Look outside the typical playdough tools to add excitement. You can use pipe cleaners and googly eyes to make monsters, sequins for sparkle, or baking accessories such as candy sprinkles and wrappers. Just give some thought to what interests your children at the moment and work that in.

OOBLECK

Oobleck, slime, goo, putty. Call it what you will. All are fun sensory takes on the same basic theme: grossness. In chapter 2, I wrote about how the biggest hook to gets kids interested in science is to pick something gross for an experiment. And this sensory recipe relies on that same basic thinking. It's icky, so kids love it. However, for those of you who try to stay away from the messes, I must say the major entertainment here comes from making the material itself, so you should absolutely loop your kids in while mixing it up. It's incredibly messy but really a huge part of this particular sensory experience. And in the realm of messes that kids make, the cleanup really isn't too bad.

Materials
- A medium mixing bowl
- 2 cups corn starch
- 2 cups water
- Food coloring
- Assorted tools (optional)

- Books about oobleck or slime (optional)
- A black light and glow-in-the-dark accessories (optional)

Directions

1. Let the kids mix the cornstarch and water in a medium-sized bowl.

2. Have the children add in food coloring.

3. Once they've mixed the ingredients together well, they can play around with adding different pressures to the mixture. It should harden when they apply pressure and turn back into more of a liquid when they ease up.

Additional Options

- Our kids will play with the oobleck itself for a long time, but you can add in some tools such as chopsticks to trace shapes and letters; and voilà—you've got hours of play time!

- Create an enjoyable literary experience with your kids by first reading a funny book about slime. (You've got many choices, but we enjoy Dr. Seuss's *Bartholomew and the Oobleck.*)

- Go spooky by adding in a glow-in-the-dark medium (such as glow-in-the-dark paint) and mixing it up in under the gleam of a black light.

WATER BEADS

Water beads are another one of those sensory projects you might find filed under, "Why would my kid want to play with those?" But trust me. Or even better, just try it. They are technically a polymer used by the floral industry, but they can be an addicting sensory play item. To use the beads, you put them in water and allow time for the beads to expand while they absorb the water. I'm not sure exactly what it is about them—maybe the shape or bright colors—but our kids seem to come up with endless play scenarios for them. From pretending they are fruit and cutting them up to make an imaginary fruit salad, to using them as pretend beads to make jewelry, they've run the gamut in our house. Our kids love to help with the water setup too, but be warned that the beads can take up to eight hours to achieve full-size, play-ready status. So don't talk them up to your kids and think you can just open the package and get started playing. You'll end up with disappointed, impatient kids. And, yes, I've done that.

Materials

- Water beads (or tapioca pearls as an alternative)
- A plastic tub or shallow tray
- Water
- Exploring accessories such as spoons, chopsticks, toothpicks, small containers
- A water table or light table (optional)

Directions

1. The directions for every brand differ slightly, but in general, you will need to place the water beads in the tray, add water, and let them sit and soak for several hours or overnight.

2. Once the water beads have fully absorbed the water, let your kids use the accessories you have chosen to explore the sensory material. Encourage them to squish, cut, sort, and just generally have fun! If you're using tapioca pearls, you can reserve some to make a kid-friendly bubble tea smoothie for a snack after play time.

Additional Options

- Our favorite take on this basic activity—especially in warmer weather—is to place a bowl of full-size water beads in the freezer overnight and find a container full of ice-encased beads in the morning! The freezing gives another sensory dimension to the activity, which adds extra fun.

- If you feel you can comfortably protect your plumbing, try adding water beads to a bathtub full of water. Our kids thought it was extremely silly to squish around a tub full of the bright things. Just make sure to strain the beads out before letting the water down the drain!

- Use them with your water table or light table for creative play. We love to add them to our outdoor water table in the summer and use the bright colors in seasonal play scenes. And they glow so pretty on the light table as well.

SAFETY NOTE

Of course, water beads are not edible, and you should use caution and your best judgment when using them with younger children. Keep them away from children who like to put things in their mouths. Another option is to use edible tapioca pearls instead.

OUTDOOR ACTIVITIES

I love doing educational, fun, and creative activities with our kids. But if we're honest with ourselves, as parents, we often spend a lot of time just trying to tire them out. Neither of my children were big nappers, and they almost always required some type of outdoor activity and fresh air to even sit still for very long. Plus I always feel better when we get out of the house for some portion of the day. It helps me to divide up our time and allows me to feel better about letting them get some unstructured play or screen time later in the afternoon if we've gone outside in the morning. And mentally I tend to do so much better when I get outdoors as well; this was especially true when they were very little.

What is available to you for outdoor activity space will obviously differ greatly depending on where you live. But if you get creative, you should be able to find outdoor space for play, which is so important for your children—and your own sanity! As I've mentioned, we lived most of our kids' young lives in the middle of a city with no green space to call our own and not really much within walking distance. But with just a little effort, we have managed to get daily, worthwhile time outside—even in bad weather.

Getting Ready for Outdoor Activities

If you have a backyard or nearby green space, then your preparation for many outdoor activities is likely very short. Several of the activities I include here are simple in that regard. But if you're looking to visit somewhere for a more organized outdoor activity, spending some time planning is worth your while. It's easy to forget, but many managed outdoor spaces require you to plan as if you were going to a museum or similar field trip. Research the spot for hours of operation and admission rates. Make sure you plan for bathroom and food options.

I've also found it helpful to consider the age and temperament of our kids in picking an appropriate outdoor activity. However, don't underestimate your child's physical ability. For example, on occasion my three-year-old would have preferred to be chauffeured about in a stroller instead of taking a small hike, but would you believe that after a few minutes of professing her total inability to "walk any farther" she started enjoying herself and forgot that her legs "didn't work"? That's what kids do. Also check the weather. Don't let rain deter you, but I've been caught with no rain gear or change of clothes on more than one occasion. Naturally, it's much better for everyone if you're prepared.

Outdoor Ideas

I use outdoor times to try to encourage self-confidence, independence, and remind my kids of what they can do on their own.

FAMILY OBSTACLE COURSE RACE

In the past several years, I've grown to love distance running. I'm not at all built for it, and running long distances usually causes my body to protest. But it's often my one chance to be alone, pushing myself, and getting fresh air. So I was hesitant to include the rest of the family. However, we had so much fun doing a family obstacle course together that I had to include it as a recommended outdoor activity. It was really great to see the kids work together and push themselves to try something new that wasn't easy. And since we've done a few races together, both kids have started trail running in the morning with me. I've embraced it as a great time to help them gain confidence by accomplishing physical (and often mental) milestones.

If you're not familiar with family obstacle course racing, these events are essentially a scaled-down version of similar adult running races with various obstacles scattered throughout a course. They are often built as looped courses—kids can run as many or as few loops as they want to reach whatever distance works best for them. They also frequently involve mud or water, but often leave a way around for kids who aren't into that. Cam was not. Many races offer some kind of swag or medal to every child who runs, which makes our kids incredibly excited. Because the events require some real space, they are often held a bit of a ways from cities. But they are held all over the country, so it's usually not difficult to find one within driving distance.

If you can't find one that works geographically or temperamentally for your kids, make one! It doesn't need to be elaborate. Our kids love to build obstacle courses for themselves (especially indoors, using every item of bedding from their rooms) and would be over the moon to help set up an outdoor situation. In the past, we've tried these activities that might work for you:

- Set up a backyard course using simple outdoor play items, such as hula hoops, skipping ropes, toy bins, and more.

- Introduce water play into the course by adding an inflatable kiddie pool. (You can include a slide too!)

- Head to an outdoor workout circuit at a local park and race each other around the trail, using the circuit stops in the race.

Creating a course at home would be a great way for the younger set to practice and get them excited for a larger family race when they get older. Plus everyone (including you) will be tired at the end; likely because you'll have carried them for some distance.

FAMILY OLYMPICS

We held our first family Olympics when Cameron was just two years old. Although I did not think it was going to rise to the level of fanfare and sportsmanship exhibited at the actual Olympic Games, I was unprepared for our extended family's raucous take and hold on the tradition developed by those first games. We are loud, we are proud, and we like to have fun. Thus, the sibling rivalry, sneak attacks, and general debauchery born that first summer have held strong, and we head into every summer with great anticipation of the next family Olympics.

Even if your family members have tamer personalities, I highly recommend working some kind of family games into your annual warm-weather repertoire. To start, kids love being involved in the planning process. They come up with the silliest and most creative concepts for games and love prepping for them. At times, we've gotten more elaborate and hung starting-line flags and purchased a dollar-store trophy. At other times, we've had a more scaled-down affair with a few simple games. But no matter what we choose to do, we have a great time planning and executing the games together.

Give some thought to the kinds of activities and games your kids and family like to do, and make sure to offer an age-appropriate take on each activity. For example, we had an egg race at our very first Olympics and Kane was upset that he was clearly the slowest and thus would not win. The whole point of the games—at least outside of the grown-up sibling rivalry among the kids' aunts, uncles, and parents—is to have fun, not to win. So we took winning out of the equation. In my experience, three to five games is generally a good number. You can incorporate whatever games you like, but here are some we like:

- Egg toss back and forth between partners, moving farther apart after each successful exchange

- Egg races on spoons

- Three-legged race, where two people team up and tie their legs together in the middle

- A whipped-cream pie tossing contest (if you can find a willing victim)

- A spinning relay race using plastic bats placed at the halfway point (Each team member runs to the bat, picks it up and holds it, and runs around it three times before running back to the start.)

Lest we sound more organized and pulled together than we actually are, it's worth pointing out that all of these events tend to devolve into total mayhem. The point is not to become so caught up in executing perfect games according to the rules that you miss out on all the excitement of just being silly together.

GEOCACHING

You might be thinking, "geo-what?" Geocaching, one of our kids' most favorite outdoor adventures, is an activity in which you use GPS (either via a GPS receiver or another mobile device) to hide and seek containers called *caches*. In plain terms, it's a real live treasure hunt. Some caches contain trinkets; other caches are the treasure in and of themselves. Our kids love it because the game doesn't really have a winner—we all work together. Sometimes we find the caches; sometimes we don't. We've been geocaching for a few years now, and we've gathered a few tips about geocaching with kids. Sign up for free on the official geocaching website (www.geocaching.com), and prep your GPS receiver or download the free geocaching app to your mobile device. Review the beginner tutorials online. We found them to be very helpful in learning how to navigate the website and use the app properly.

Plan ahead by looking on the website for your intended caches. You can browse by postal code if you plan to search farther from your home, or have the site look for caches close to you

based on your current location. Once you've done it a few times, feel free to look when you're already out and about. Our kids turn waiting time for anything into "do we have time to look for a geocache?"

Pick the best caches for your children's ages. Caches are organized by size and type, difficulty in terrain, and level of seeking difficulty. We have found that the best for us are traditional caches of regular or large size. These are quite rare in metropolitan areas, so be willing to look for some nano caches if that's where you're starting! I also like to check the description of caches and hints ahead of time to gauge if it's going to be too tricky for us to find. Also check for the last date the particular cache was found; it's a good sign if someone found it recently!

Be prepared for larger caches and bring as many trinkets as you plan on taking from the cache. I'd also recommend hand wipes and hand sanitizer—it's a dirty business.

We are huge fans of geocaching, but I'd definitely characterize it as a divisive activity. You either love it or hate it. I've had plenty of friends join in on the activity, only to be driven mad trying to find a cache or disgusted by some of the grimy things left inside. In my opinion, if you think your kids might like hunting for treasure (a term I use incredibly loosely) and enjoy the hunt just as much as finding any actual treasure, I highly recommend checking it out!

GLAMPING

I like to say that I grew up spending my summers in a vacation scenario even more rustic than camping. My family owns a cabin on a small island in Lake Michigan; the cabin is 130 square feet and has no running water or electricity. We went every summer from when I was three years old until high school, when my parents could no longer drag us up there. It was simple, but the source of so many good memories and creative times with my own family. I finally took my husband and our kids up there one recent summer—although they didn't go for staying in the cabin. We rented a bigger, more modernized home. But our kids instantly took to the same things I loved, and it was an incredibly special experience.

Based on that, you may think I love camping, right? Nope, I don't. And my husband really doesn't. But Kane and Cameron were relentless in asking us to take them camping. So I started our own form that we call *glamping*. And by *glam*, I don't mean sipping champagne by a fire built by someone else, nestled all snuggly in colorful Hudson blankets. I mean putting a tent in the yard so that we have somewhere to go to the bathroom and a warm bed to escape to in the middle of the night when someone inevitably is no longer interested in sleeping on the ground.

The kids love it and it's easy enough, so we do it almost every summer. To keep everyone happy, I suggest keeping your eye on the weather before picking an evening to sleep out. Then have your kids help gather camping items—a tent, sleeping bags, flashlights, some comfy stuffed animals, a few nature books, and so on. Depending on how old your kids are, try to have them help set up a tent. (For those of you who have done real camping, this tends to be a much less stressful process than when you are trying to do it in the middle of woods before nightfall.) Get the tents all comfy, and then wait until dusk. We head out just shortly before bedtime and get everyone tucked in, read a few books, talk about the stars and nature sounds we hear, and then my kids are usually worn out and sleep through the night. It sounds silly, but they love it.

HIKING AND NATURE CENTERS

We are also big fans of simply taking a hike, a term I use loosely to mean a walk outdoors. When the kids were very young and still required strollers, I'd look for a nature center or park that had some form of paved walking loop. I've found the visitor centers at most places to be a good resource for identifying which trails might be easy and interesting for kids as well (typically small loops starting with lots of things to see along the way). But make sure to keep in mind your comfort level with the children in whatever green space you're visiting. I vividly remember taking the kids (when they were only two and three) by myself to a wetland and cringing nervously as they ran down planked walkways spanning over open water. Despite the fact that the water was probably only a few feet deep (if that), I might have screamed for the kids to "sit down," "don't move," and "enjoy the nature" so much that the fun was taken out of it. We all have our bad days and limits, and it's good to be aware of those. But if you love the outdoors and real hiking, go for it!

Before you even set out on a trail, give serious thought to your kids' ages, as well as the length and difficulty of hiking routes they can handle. I am all for pushing kids a little. But in contrast to my approach to many other activities in this book, I try to underestimate their hiking ability, especially when they're young. It's not pleasant to have to haul your kids back on a trail because they couldn't complete the hike. If you underestimate, the worst thing that will happen is that you learn that they can actually go farther. Then maybe you extend the hike a bit the next time.

I also try to plan ahead for a few things we can do while hiking. I personally enjoy the peace and quiet of a good walk in the woods, but my kids are known for complaining about just "walking for no reason." Your related activities don't have to be elaborate. You could teach them about trail markers, keep your eyes peeled for a certain animal or plant, or play out a story. Think about what interests your kids, and then find a way to loop that in.

Even parents of exuberant children can count on the fact that their kids will get tired at some point along a hike and need to rest. To avoid the situation where our kids are splayed out on the ground whining, I try to plan for rest time and think of little quiet activities we can do. If you know interesting landmarks can be found along the way, plan to stop there and discuss them. Or stop to do a little nature-themed art with things you find on the ground—rock and leaf mosaics are a favorite of ours. Stopping for snacks and drinks is also a good idea. And if there is a nature center near the hike, plan on stopping there at the end. Your kids will have something to look forward to, pushing them on, and it doubles as a good recuperating time at the end of a hike (and usually a good bathroom break).

I SPY

I Spy is a classic, easy game, and I think that we all love it because it is so adaptable to whatever interests our kids at the moment. And you can keep it simple or make it more challenging as your kids get older. Typically, the game is played by a person spotting an object and describing it to the group using one characteristic, such as, "I spy something green." Then everyone looks around to see if they can spot the object. And we take this classic approach often enough. But we also like to turn I Spy into more of a treasure hunt when we're outside. And when done in that way, I find that it's a wonderful educational activity that provokes conversation while incorporating our kids' interests and keeping them active outside.

To begin, spend some time thinking about your particular child's interests. Do they like cars? Put together a little bag of toy cars and have them go spying for similar models or colors on a walk. Are colors their thing? Go on a Rainbow I Spy hunt about town. Whatever it is, focus on what your kids like—I promise you will hold their interest and get them excited. Need some ideas to get started? Here are three of our favorite ways to play outside:

- Nature I Spy—Come up with a list ahead of time, and you can even print out photos of items in nature to use as reference. We took a hysterical Nature I Spy walk around the city a few years ago, and the kids were really stretching their imaginations to find objects that qualified. (For example, a three-year-old Kane insisted that a bird on a street mural counted as an actual bird.) It's a great way to get kids to notice nature, whether you're in the middle of it or not!

- Urban I Spy—This one was born of the fact that our Nature I Spy game around the neighborhood took entirely too long. We came up with our own Urban I Spy game (free cards are available to download on the blog if you search for "I spy"), and you can too! Enlist your kids to help come up with objects that are unique to your neighborhood or city, and then set out to find them.

- Letter or Number I Spy—This is a perfect game for those reluctant readers and mathematicians. I highly recommend making a checklist of numbers and letters for this one. It's a good way to reinforce both letters and numbers and to hold the kids accountable (in a gentle way) for actually knowing them. To make it even more fun, turn it into a bingo game. It does not need to be fancy. Just draw simple cards with letters or numbers on them, and use stickers to mark your finds. (We also have free downloadable Letter and Number Hunt Bingo cards available on the blog if you search for "bingo.")

OUTDOOR ART WALK OR SCULPTURE GARDEN

This outdoor activity is slightly more dependent on where you live, but as with so many of the activities discussed in this book, I've always found some form of outdoor art everywhere we've been. Regardless of the quality or whether you love the particular art, it's a really wonderful way to introduce the concept of visiting art museums without the pressure of being indoors.

Activities are just naturally more relaxed in the outdoor setting. Plus depending on the rules of the particular space, kids are even allowed to touch some of the art.

If you live in or near a metropolitan area, chances are that there is an art museum with some outdoor art component. I've often also found that many outdoor destinations, such as maintained gardens or historical homes, have temporary or permanent art exhibits outdoors. If you do a little research, you'll see what is available in your area. We often visit outdoor art destinations when I simply need to give the kids some space to roam and want some visual interest along the way. But when it seems like a good fit, I'll try to work in a variety of activities. Here are some possibilities:

- Try story playing about the art you see. For example, we'll imagine that a winged statue is going to take flight and tell a story about where it would go and what it would do. Sometimes we'll also bring a favorite book with us, read a few chapters, and act out a story from the book in the space. (When we took a trip to local Dumbarton Oaks' sculpture garden, we read a few spooky chapters from a book about mummies and set off in search of some amidst the statues.)

- Bring along a simple sketchbook with pencils, paints, or pens, and have the kids draw a bit of what they see. It's a great way to have kids spend a discrete amount of time focused on art with a very easy, active escape nearby.

- Play I Spy! This is a cool activity for any art setting. Depending on the type of art in your outdoor location, go out looking for a certain object (animals are a favorite), art medium (bronze), or story type (Greek mythology). This game is a great way to get kids moving around and engaged!

FIELD TRIPS

As the name of my blog might suggest, I have a serious need to get out and about. No doubt, we have days that we spend entirely at home doing arts and crafts projects, but I find that everyone stays happier when we have a good balance of field trips mixed in. This was especially the case when our kids were very young and had not started any real version of school yet. I hated feeling trapped inside all day long, even if I could think of an endless number of projects for us all to do. Fresh air and interaction with other people (for all of us) is a must. And I find that getting out and seeing things in action (art, science, and so on) really helps round out and reinforce all the activities we do at home and now also at school.

Now I know that we happen to be quite fortunate to live in a city where there are many museums, art galleries, and historic places to visit (and most of those are free to visit as well). I could suggest that you all just move to

Washington, DC, but there is no need. With a little research and planning, I've found some form of field trip in almost every place we have ever visited (including smaller towns and remote islands). Use your imagination—it doesn't have to be an outing to a Smithsonian museum to count as an educational, fun trip. Sometimes our best field trips have been to random places. I find that we always learn something, even if it's not what I intended when I planned the outing.

My general approach is to think of something exciting and interesting first and then look for the educational angle second. The spot doesn't necessarily have to be educationally oriented to serve as a learning opportunity. And, no big surprise here—I think it's fine to pick something that I find enjoyable and intriguing, even if my kids have no idea of what it is yet. Now that the kids are older, I try to pick an outing that ties into something they are doing at school, which can be as simple as looking at colors at an art museum. Or I'll do a follow-up to an activity we've done at home, such as a trip with some connection to a historical event we read about. But honestly, my overall goal is simply just to get us out of the house!

Preparing for Field Trips

Out of all of the activities we do, I probably put the most planning time into preparing for field trips. I keep a list of places we'd like to visit and check ahead of time for hours of operation, exhibits, rates, discounts, membership opportunities, and food options.

Once you've picked a place, make some time in advance to talk to your kids about the trip. Even when our kids were really young toddlers, I would discuss with them ahead of time what my behavioral expectations for them were. We continue to have those discussions even now that they are a bit older and have visited lots of places. That conversation changes over time and is always completely distinct from their actual behavior—they don't always meet my expectations. And I have my good and bad days too. But each time we make a trip, their overall ability to behave generally improves. If we are going to an art museum, we discuss at length about not touching art, keeping voices low, and not running around. And if we are going somewhere more interactive, which I really try to balance out with the other places that require more controlled behavior, I let them know ahead of time that they should feel free to touch whatever they want, ask as many questions as they can come up with, but still stick close by me.

At the heart of all trips, I remember that I know our kids. I know what they can handle, and I know that the more places we visit, the better they get at visiting and the more they get out of it. So don't be dissuaded by what other people think is appropriate for your kids. I once took a three-and-a-half-year-old Cameron to a favorite modern art museum, the Hirshhorn, to see Ai Weiwei's exhibit of fabulous sculptures using everyday objects. We'd visited many times before and Cam knew that she wasn't supposed to cross the sparkly line delineating the sculpture from the viewing area. Despite my telling the security guard this, he basically followed her around the entire exhibit, constantly reminding her to stay away from the lines. She walked right up to the line around a sculptural piece made entirely of loose tea leaves and sat down to look. As the guard stood right near us, laser-eyeing Cam, he totally missed the adult walking past the line and into the sculpture, spreading the tea leaves everywhere. As the alarm sounded, I could not keep the smirk off of my face. I know he was just doing his job, but I know our kids.

> I know what they can handle, and I know that the more places we visit, the better they get at visiting and the more they get out of it. So don't be dissuaded by what other people think is appropriate for your kids.

And you know yours, so try not to let others' expectations of what kids can do prevent you from taking a trip. If they do misbehave, you should not feel as though you made a mistake by taking them to an adult place. They are kids and, as shown by our Hirshhorn visit, even adults make mistakes. But this is how children learn, or at least you learn that they may not be ready for something yet. And that is generally where I find the pretrip snack planning to come in handy; a quick escape for sustenance is sometimes necessary.

Field Trip Ideas

As I mentioned, we live in a metropolitan area with easy access to lots and lots of field trips. But a field trip does not have to involve visiting a world-famous art museum to get you out of the house, entertain your children, stir up creativity, or teach your kids something new. So try to think outside the box and be willing to travel a bit. I'm honestly not the most optimistic person in the world, but I can probably count on one hand the number of times we've returned from an outing thinking, "Well, that was a waste of time." That's a different thought from "Well, that was a total disaster," which is a thought I've had many more times. Even if all you get out of visiting a random place is a funny story and time between naps used up, you probably won't regret it. To get you started, I've included the best types of field trips we've experienced, my approach to visiting each place, and the kinds of activities we like to do when we visit. Of course, you will have to pick a place that makes sense geographically for you, and remember to take into account your family's interests, but I highly suggest just jumping on in. What's the worst that could happen? You discover that your kids don't like it? Then it's on to the next one!

ART MUSEUM OR GALLERY

As I'm sure you've surmised by now, we spend a lot of our time doing art-related activities, which is definitely a big function of the fact that I really like art. But I also think it's because kids are so incredibly open to art when they are young. They like knowing that there is no wrong or right way to create art, and so our kids have always enjoyed visiting art museums or galleries.

Before we go, I like to spend some time ahead looking online at the museum or gallery, perusing the exhibits, and picking out artists that match up to our kids' interests. For example, we went to a Lichtenstein pop art comic book exhibit for Kane and a costume wear exhibit for Cameron. We visit with the presumption that the kids will have the stamina and focus for one or maybe two exhibits. Depending on the cost of the visit, I might push for a little more time spent there, but it is important to know the limits of your kids' attention spans when it comes to art. If visiting for a short period of time isn't going to work out, we try to either take turns with the kids at certain exhibits or work in some play and eating time in the middle of our visit. (Many museum admissions are good for a full day and allow you to leave and return.) And don't forget about yourself! If you like a particular type of art but your kids aren't that interested in it, there's nothing wrong with telling them that you get a turn too.

If you have access to modern or more nontraditional art museums, they can be great for very young kids because the artwork they see looks a lot like the artwork they make. In no way do I mean to disparage modern or self-trained artists—I don't actually think, "My three-year-old could make that"—but I've found that our kids seemed to enjoy that type of art more when they were very little. Also modern art is just my favorite. As the kids get a little older and more verbal, more traditional art museums become more fun, as they can pick out and discuss subjects related to the art.

As I suggested in the beginning of this section, before you visit a museum, talk with your children about museum behavior and not touching works of art and why. I often found it hard to visit art museums with both kids when they were very little, so I would try to take one at a time or at least have one in a carrier or stroller. If a museum has a more interactive area, where they can explore and touch things, I like to take our kids there first (such

as a fountain or a sculpture garden where that's permissible) and then keep our time in more restricted areas limited with plenty of run-free time afterward. But even with all that planning, realize that your kids aren't going to behave as an adult would. Try not to take it personally that some adults don't like having children there. My feeling is that as long as our kids are behaving appropriately for their ages and being respectful (while learning how to actually do those very things), then I don't pay much attention to what others think.

Once you're there, make sure to make it interesting for the children. They will pick up the serious parts of art too. If that's all you focus on, however, it's not going to be enjoyable for anyone. To that end, I like to look online and ask museum docents upon arrival whether they have any special activities available for children and families. Even if the activity is for slightly older children, I find that they give me ideas of things to do with our kids when we visit. If not, I've got plenty of ideas for you to start with!

- Bring a small sketchbook and drawing tools (probably colored pencils and not permanent markers) and give your kids an opportunity to sketch in front of artwork. You can ask them to draw what they see, or you can just see what they come up with on their own.

- Ahead of time, draft a list of descriptive words to use in discussing art. While you're at the museum, use them to talk about the works of art and encourage your kids to use them also. You don't need to get fancy or technically advanced; words and concepts as simple as *happy, fast,* or *bright* get the conversation going. Or just ask them what they see—you'll be surprised at what they say!

- If your kids are reticent to give their own ideas or are having a hard time getting interested in the art, suggest a game of I Spy. In modern art museums, we play the game by looking for colors, shapes, techniques, or media (such as a collage, sculpture, or painting). In more traditional art museums, we look for subjects in the artwork that match up to our children's interests. Kane likes to look for knights in armor or aspects of ancient civilizations; Cam loves to look for animals or activities she enjoys, such as swimming.

I use all of these activities on a regular basis to encourage the kids to appreciate art. Although at times my strategies work better than at others, I've noticed that both kids get better and better each time we visit art museums at actually looking at, thinking about, and discussing the art.

GREEN SPACE

Whether you live in the middle of a big city, further out in a suburb, or on a giant rural farm, making time to spend in green space is a must. Frankly, with so many different kinds of green

spaces to explore, you have no excuse not to. A park, arboretum, botanical gardens, nature preserve, or simply an open field can all provide a great space for kids. To be fair, while living in a city affords us easy access to wonderful museums, we definitely have to work a bit to find great green spaces. For most of our kids' lives, I couldn't just open up our back door to let the kids roam free. For me, play time in green spaces took a little planning. Even if you do have a giant backyard, it's helpful to spend some time in other green space with purpose. While I love to let our kids out to play a bit by themselves, intentionally visiting green space keeps me more involved. Over the years, we've developed a good list of our favorite spots to play outdoors. Yet I still try to plan ahead, reviewing a site map where available and picking out one or two areas I think our kids would most enjoy. I've found that many parks and nature preserves have a few areas designed specifically for kids, such as a children's garden, so those are great places to start.

Sometimes we visit a green space just for the sake of running wild and free for a bit. But if I want to visit a more confined area with the kids for a particular reason—for example, the holiday exhibit at the Botanical Gardens or the Bonsai Museum at the National Arboretum—I always look for lots of open space to run and play after touring those particular exhibits. Just as with our visits to art museums, I make sure that there is somewhere afterward with quick access for free play time. Plus, snacks. Lots of snacks. For everyone involved.

Not specific enough for you? Well, don't worry. We have some great activities for spending time in green space that I'm happy to share.

By far, the go-to outdoor activity for our kids is story playing. Sometimes they make up a story, and occasionally we bring a book with us to read in the outdoors. But I find that when they play out a story, it provides a creative way for them to get some exercise and incorporate the natural world into their imaginations. Although I'll play along, I also find that the kids will pick up a story and literally run with it by themselves, leaving me to enjoy some outdoor time almost to myself.

Similar to story playing, I like to connect our time spent in green space with other activities our kids are doing at home or at school. For example, we might collect natural objects (where allowed) for an art project. Or we might bring some messy science project outdoors with us. When Kane and Cameron were very little, we would play I Spy to look for colors or even play an alphabet game with park signs. Whatever the connection we make, I find that doing so outdoors reinforces things they're learning elsewhere in a fun and different way. And it also helps out in those inevitable situations where at least one child is hungry, has to go to the bathroom, hates nature that particular day, or has some other difficulty, and needs to be distracted by connecting what you're doing to something else they enjoy. Did I mention you're going to need to bring lots of snacks?

HISTORIC SITE OR MUSEUM

I'm pretty much the furthest thing from a history buff you'll find, so I think it's incredibly comical that both of our children express a real interest in the subject. I honestly just don't have a knack for remembering historical events, dates, names, or facts. Our kids absolutely got that from their father. I've become quite the visitor of historic sites and museums, however, because I'm frequently the one leading the field trips. Sometimes it's good to force yourself to do things you don't necessarily like to do, especially when it's something your kids are interested in, and you can show the kids that education is a lifelong process. In the beginning, our kids still considered me an authority on everything and would continually ask me historically related questions. But ever since they witnessed a frantic Googling effort on my part during a trip to Colonial Williamsburg in Virginia, when I was trying to explain why we were passing all sorts of Civil War battlefields on our way to a Revolutionary War site, they've good naturedly accepted that we are all in the education effort together.

Moreover, I find it very easy to discover activities at a broad range of historical sites and museums that suit all of our particular personalities. Historical field trips offer a bevy of activities—including straight-up lectures, culinary adventures, and interactive arts—that balance out tours and truly provide something for everyone. You won't find everything at every place you visit, so absolutely look ahead of time and do some planning to decide if a particular historical trip is a good fit for your family. It also helps to determine what you would like to concentrate on during your visit; for example, on our trip to Williamsburg, we found a sword fighting demonstration for Kane, a dance lesson for Cameron, and spoon bread from a tavern for me. But don't dismiss historically related field trips outright as boring. Even this incredibly amateur historian has had a lot of fun visiting and learning at each place we've gone. And keep in mind, as I pointed out in the discussion on art museums, historic sites and museums do not need to be epic to warrant a visit. Everywhere has a history—explore it!

In addition to having a range of subject matter activities that allow you to check out different aspects of a historical place, I think museums and historical sites make for some of the best field trips because almost all of them have something specifically geared toward children. Check online ahead of time and plan on visiting those activities at a bigger museum first, before they get too busy. But if a child-specific activity isn't offered, I like to tie our visit to a book we have read or a movie we have seen (both of which are great ways to give these visits context when read or viewed ahead of time). I find that it really helps bring subjects that we've discussed to life and reinforces concepts for all of us when we've seen and experienced firsthand the activities from a particular time period.

For example, we found ourselves on a trip down a total historical rabbit hole after a visit to the Library of Congress (which was a great historical place to visit). Always a lover of conspiracy

theories, I thought Kane would enjoy watching the *National Treasure* movies, which prominently feature the Library of Congress. Upon watching them, both kids immediately became interested in the Freemasons. So we took a follow-up field trip to check out a local Masonic temple and had a fantastically interesting tour. One thing kept leading to another, and before we knew it, we were geocaching for Masonic treasure ourselves! Most of all, it helped the kids learn something about important historical figures that they might not otherwise have gleaned simply from reading a book. I love when I come across intriguing hooks and we have these spontaneous learning moments. I don't really have a good recipe for finding such unexpected moments, but I can say that the more things we do, the more often they happen. And you thought history was boring!

Also perhaps because I'm also on an educational quest on these visits, historical field trips are one of my favorite ways to grow our kids' self-confidence by encouraging them to interact with staff. The kid-centered activities are absolutely primed for it, and I've found almost all staff at historical sites to be approachable and excited about sharing information with kids. If we run into a more challenging personality, I find that teaching kids to interact with less approachable people and to be politely persistent are also good skills to learn. Kane needs very little encouragement to speak up, and he sort of thinks as he speaks. Cameron, however, is more on the reflective side. But I've found that historical field trips offer an opportunity to help her speak

up. For example, the National Park Service's Junior Ranger program encourages children to seek out information and interact with park staff in order to earn a badge from a particular site. A four-year-old Cam worked really hard and pushed herself to ask and answer questions from a park ranger to earn her badge at the Antietam Battlefield site. Again, consider your child's personality, but I think helping kids to build self-confidence by gently pushing them beyond their comfort point is important, and historical field trips provide an excellent opportunity to do just that.

MUSIC SHOW

Now, history might not be my strong suit, but I have always been a big fan of music and am interested in a fairly wide range of genres. But I'll admit that I was somewhat unprepared for the almost cult followings many kids' musical groups have. And I'm not just talking about the kids. In fact, it's really the parents' reliving of their own music show days that seems to drive it. When we attended one show put on by a nationally popular kids band, parents were literally elbowing their way to get front row seats (on the floor) and yelling out song requests as if they were shouting, "Play 'Free Bird'!" I scoffed, naturally. A few years later, however, I found myself singing my heart out to Recess Monkey's live performance of "Flapjacks," dancing like a fool, and telling the band I used to live in Seattle too. Even four-year-old Kane knew to be

embarrassed by my behavior. All of which I share as an introduction to tell you that music shows are another great way to entertain your children while keeping up your own interests.

Music shows are fun, they get kids moving, and they can be educational. Some kids' bands come up with incredibly clever educational lyrics that the children actually remember because they're set to music. So how should you break into the kids' music scene? I've had the best success with taking our kids to shows where we spend some time listening to the group's music before attending. Our kids get really excited when they hear something they recognize and like to sing along. Where it's allowed, particularly for really young toddlers, I also like to bring instruments for the kids to play along—nothing that would distract the band, but something entertaining that helps the kids feel like a part of the performance.

In addition, give some thought to the type of music and venue and whether those align with your particular children's personalities. Like many children, our kids do the best at outdoor events, where there is room to move around while listening. Kids' bands are obvious choices, but consider other musical genres that are family friendly and might also work well for children. For example, we attended an outdoor jazz concert with the kids in Chicago one year and both of them were riveted. Because it was outside, we were able to find an area where the kids could listen but still move around and make noise without disturbing other listeners. If you can find free shows—many towns and cities have free music series in the summer—even better. I don't feel quite so bad if our kids are slightly intruding on others' listening experiences when the show is free.

No matter the venue, though, make sure you think about your children's feelings about loud music. Some bands tone the sound level down for kids, but many turn it way, way up. Similarly, some children are enthralled by extremely loud sounds, but equally as common are children scared by higher noise levels. Cameron loves to jam out to loud music, but Kane gets very skittish around it and wants to sit way, way back or even leave occasionally. The noise level is one thing I never push them on. I want them to be comfortable and have fun.

Last, one of things I love most about attending kids' music shows is the opportunity to meet the band after. Not all bands offer this option. For those who do, it's a really great way to encourage children's confidence by providing them an opportunity to speak with adults about an easy subject. Who doesn't love meeting a rock star?

PUBLIC TRANSPORTATION

Whether or not your children are obsessed with cars, trains, or buses, taking public transportation to nowhere in particular makes for an excellent field trip. We take public transportation simply as a means to get other places as well, but both of our kids always seem to enjoy taking a ride as an end in and of itself. And I love that the trips can be a low-key way to get out of the house and just let the kids take in the sights. Plus, public transportation is generally reasonably priced and usually free for young children. Buses and trains are the obvious choices, but think outside the box a bit. If you live or are traveling anywhere near water, see if there's a ferry running. Some of our most favorite rides to nowhere have been on ferries, which offer a completely different travel experience than other forms of public transportation. Not technically public transportation and certainly more expensive, other forms of transportation such as taxis or sightseeing tours on double-decker buses or boats can get the kids incredibly excited. So keep those in mind as another option to get out and about.

Depending on where you live, the degree to which you need to locate and plan ahead to take a ride will vary. But in general, I find it helpful to check routes and schedules ahead of time. Keep in mind that food and drink often can't be consumed on public transportation, so build in some snack time off route—even if it's just hopping off at a stop to have snacks you've packed. If you're taking young kids who need a stroller, look for accessibility in advance—not all stops along routes have elevators, and it's no fun to find that out the hard way. Also turnstiles of any kind are more difficult with strollers, which is good to remember if you're ever taking the New York subway. Speaking from personal experience, nothing screams tourist more than getting stuck in a turnstile with two young children and a giant stroller while trying to catch the A Train.

As I mentioned, I love transportation field trips because they often provide a low-key way to take in sights. Young children are just excited to look out the window at whatever is whizzing by, especially other vehicles. But if you have older kids, or your little ones tire of just looking around, you can explore a whole host of activities on your ride:

- Talk about how the vehicle you're riding works. Cameron loves to figure out how things work. Depending on your level of knowledge about the subject and the age of your child, you can keep the discussion basic or stretch it to a more scientific or engineering level. Because my general level of knowledge about all things mechanical is very elementary, questions lobbed by our kids have frequently spurred library field trips to check out books about whatever transport we were taking at the time.

- Use it as an exercise to teach about fundamental concepts such as money (let your kids help purchase fare cards); time (Kane loves to help determine when the next train or bus is coming); or social interaction (for example, giving a seat to those who need it most).

- Play any kind of I Spy that strikes your fancy. Look for letters, colors, numbers, kinds of buildings, or even types of jobs (business person, postal worker, and so on). If you really want to make an interesting game of it, put together a set of I Spy cards to use. You can find lots of nature sets available for free online, or you can download our tongue-in-cheek Urban I Spy cards from our blog (search for "urban I spy" and look for the link to the Google doc) if you live in a more urban area. (Feral cats are much more prolific in the city than many nature items are.)

Sometimes you may also just need a bit of time to take a seat and stop chasing your kids around; that works well too. You never know—everyone might get a little rest on the ride.

SCIENCE MUSEUM

I'm sure it's obvious by now, but I'm a little bit of a science nerd, so one field trip that really gets my excitement level up is taking the kids to explore new science museums. I've always learned better by reading and reflection, but you really can't beat learning science by physically exploring the concepts yourself. Even if your toddler won't fully understand Newton's Law of Gravity, I guarantee kids this age will like dropping things and pushing things off of tables. And most science museums do a great job of setting up exhibits for children to have fun exploring science in a hands-on, interactive way. If you're lucky, you might even see a real scientist working on something, which always excites my kids.

As with visiting other types of museums, I highly recommend checking ahead of time for exhibits that your kids might enjoy, particularly if there are any current special exhibits. Those tend to get crowded quickly, so head there first. Many science museums also offer kid-friendly activities throughout the day, which might not be posted ahead of time and also may have a capped number of participants requiring sign-up. So check in at the front desk when you arrive. Spend some time thinking about your children's interest in particular areas of science and their ability to listen to material read aloud to them—many science museums contain a large amount of information, but the kids will either need to read or listen to it being read to them. I like to

make sure to intersperse activity-related exhibits with those that require reading or listening. And snack breaks and outdoor time always help too.

Even if the museum doesn't offer child-specific activities, you can find so many different interesting options for all age groups to incorporate into your visit:

- Make a science notebook at home and write down scientific questions as they come up. You can then use these questions as a way to explore the museum and try to answer them. Questions don't need to be elaborate—something as simple as, "Why does it rain?" can easily be explored during a visit. And if you have one of those inquiring children, this can be a great way to actually get his questions answered.

- Help your kids build self-confidence by encouraging them to speak with museum staff, ask questions, and offer their own opinions about what they are seeing. I've found that science museum staff members are generous about engaging with children.

- Follow up on scientific principles you learn at the museum by conducting your own experiments soon after. Then the science lesson tends to stick a little better. If you don't like to get messy at home, some science museums offer hands-on experiments on-site, which can provide the perfect opportunity for your children to learn without you losing your mind over bubbling science explorations in your kitchen.

As always, try to just go with it. We have definitely had those visits where I wanted to take our kids to see a special exhibit, but they decided they would rather stay in a water exploration room for four hours. It can be frustrating if you've paid a museum fee and had a plan in mind, but try not to get too stuck!

THEATER

Plenty of parents cringe at the thought of trying to get their young child to sit quietly and patiently while watching a theater performance. It's one of those field-trip activities that set parents up to feel as though they are onstage as well—to get their child to behave, that is. But I quickly got over that, and I hope you will too. Most areas have a broad range of theater programs for kids to attend—whether the child is capable of sitting for a full-length play or not. These programs can help stimulate imagination, grow listening skills, and encourage self-discipline.

When picking what type of show to take our youngest to, I've had to check my own interests at the door a bit. For example, many young kids gravitate toward puppet shows, which would not be on the top of my list for entertainment. But I realized that introducing them to the theater this way could be worth putting my own interests aside. And I'd recommend that you do the same. For really young kids, look for a children's theater or family programs at a regular theater, including performances that adjust lighting and sound for young audience members. While it's easy to pop in and out of museums, it can be difficult to cut theater performances short (although I've certainly done it). So I consider it best to build on theater going slowly—starting with shorter programs put together especially for younger children, and then working your way up to longer programs with intermissions built in.

Where possible, try to find a theater performance that has some interactive element to it. We've been to kids shows where performers solicited ideas from audience members or even allowed the kids to come up on stage. All of those make for a more fun and confidence-building experience. If you live close to a theater that does performances for adults, check to see if they give any public access to dress rehearsals. We had the opportunity to attend a dress rehearsal of the Shakespeare Theater's *Henry V,* which provided a low-key way for the kids to experience a more grown-up theater performance and get an awesome behind-the-scenes look at theater itself. Plus the director spoke directly to the public throughout, which made for a great interactive experience. You might also check out festivals that are theater in and of themselves. At some Renaissance festivals you can even rent costumes, so they can provide a fantastic way for kids to get in on the drama.

In terms of activities, I find that attending theater performances is less about things we do during the show than other field trips, but you can add on before and after to get more out of the experience:

- If the performance is based on a book or story, read it first! Although some kids like to be surprised, many more like to know what's going to happen and will feel more comfortable during a performance if they're familiar with the plot and characters.

- Spend some time learning about theater concepts—such as set design, costumes, and dialogue—before the performance. While you're waiting for the show to start, look together at the set (if you can) and point out some of the things you've learned. Do the same at the end of the play for other theater concepts.

- Help your children translate the story you saw into their own play at home! It can be a simple puppet show or a more elaborate performance, but both of our kids love reenacting scenes from theater performances we've attended. Dressing up adds to the excitement!

ZOO OR AQUARIUM

It just so happens that alphabetically, this section falls last on my list of field trip activities. For a variety of reasons, it is also probably my least favorite among the types of trips we take. Putting aside all sorts of animal welfare issues, zoos and aquariums tend to be crowded, and I often find it difficult to actually learn anything. They can also be expensive, especially the aquariums. Moreover, our kids seem almost desensitized to the exhibits because there are so many distractions (for example, wanting to get their faces painted instead of looking at the awesome lion). And personally, I do not like big crowds. However, I do think kids enjoy them and they offer a good amount of space for children to roam. Although I encourage field trips that take into account your own interests, these trips aren't all about me. Plus we've been

able to find some kind of zoo or aquarium almost any place we've ever visited, so it's a great idea to keep in your back pocket when traveling.

My number-one recommendation for zoos or aquariums, especially if you are thinking of visiting a local one or have some flexibility in timing, is to call or visit the facility and ask outright when the peak visiting times are, and then avoid them. It is frustrating for all involved to be shuttled and shoved around and then not even see any animals. When you arrive, check at the visitor's center to see what is going on that day and ask for tips on what times are best to view particular animals.

MEMBERSHIP CAN PAY OFF

Much like science museums, you can get reciprocal membership opportunities when you join a zoo or aquarium belonging to the Association of Zoos and Aquariums. I've found that becoming a member at one often pays for itself after just a few visits and often entitles you to early previews of new exhibits and other special membership benefits. It's definitely worth checking out if you are going to be taking a large group with you.

For example, the National Zoo in Washington, DC, has these awesome outdoor orangutan lines that allow visitors to watch the apes swing and climb their way along an overhead obstacle course between buildings. But the orangutans only have access to the "O Line" at certain times of day, and even that depends on the weather. To avoid getting stuck waiting endlessly for something that's not going to happen, I check to see what is planned for that particular day. Even if there aren't special events going on, some animals are just more active at certain times of day, and it's worth knowing that as well. Try not to become too scheduled, however. You may think you've got all the timing down pat, and then the kids want to spend an hour watching meerkats. (And really, who doesn't?) If that means you miss a sea lion feeding, so be it.

Whether you are a scheduler or not, I would definitely check ahead online or at the visitor's center when you arrive for any special kid-related activities or areas. Interactive, hands-on exhibits for kids can make the visit so much more interesting. Also many zoos and aquariums have some type of play area set up for children, which can be so helpful. Depending on the moods of our kids, I generally head straight to the exhibits while their attention span is strong and take a play break when they start to fade. Many of the play areas involve water play, which means your kids are likely to get soaked from head to toe. So if you'd like to keep spirits high afterward, have a nice, dry set of clothes to change into. Speaking of keeping spirits high, it helps to have plenty of snacks or a packed meal. Zoo and aquarium cafeterias are notoriously expensive and overcrowded.

Perhaps they just don't spark my creativity as much, but I find that zoos and aquariums don't naturally lend themselves to the same array of activities as other trips do. That being said, I've still got a regular rotation of activities up my sleeve for these types of visits:

- Try adventure story playing. Pretend you are explorers or on a viewing safari, out tracking wild animals, and see who can gather the most information about a particular animal.

- Play I Spy for an animal your child loves or knows from a book, television show, or movie. Kane once insisted that a group of fish labeled "pilchards" were actually sardines because they were swimming in a particular school formation. Turns out he was right— and he learned it from one of his favorite shows: *Octonauts*. So we kept looking for more aquatic life from the show as a modified I Spy. We also like to play Rainbow I Spy or get the kids to focus on the exhibit captions by reading them together for Alphabet I Spy.

- Pick one group of animals or aquatic life that you've studied at home or in school and try to find examples of what you've learned.

And when all else fails, just let them run around. Zoos and aquariums are full of kids being kids, so at least take the opportunity to let them do that.

AFTERWORD

Are you still with me? I know that was a lot of information, but I hope you have gained ideas about focusing on where your interests lie and have some creative thoughts of your own starting to percolate. As I mentioned in the beginning, my whole point here is not to create a step-by-step, cookie-cutter plan for finding fun with your kids and keeping your sanity. I wish I could help you out, but that just doesn't exist. Rather, my goal is start you thinking of your own ideas to find a balance between keeping you and your kids engaged and entertained. As I noted earlier, I like to think of my own process in three stages:

1. Look first at activities you like yourself.

2. Consider your own personality in looking for new interests.

3. Take whatever activity you've picked, and adapt it to work with your own child's personality and interests.

Above all, focus on process and not product. I hope you find something that works well for you and your family and share it with others too!

RESOURCES

Art, Craft, and Science Suppliers

ONLINE SUPPLIERS

We purchase almost all of our art, craft, and science supplies online. It can take some trial and error to become equipped with the optimal size and scale of supplies. (I might have purchased 200 tiny apple containers once with the intent of filling them with apple playdough, and I'm pretty sure we still have 198 left.) But once you get your needs sorted out, ordering online is the way to go if you have access to the Internet. I don't know if you've ever taken your children to

an art or craft store, but I find it even worse than taking them to the grocery store. They want absolutely everything! So I keep my eye on online suppliers for deals and free shipping offers. This list is by no means exhaustive, but here are some sites that work well for me and a few of the supplies I like best from each.

Amazon (http://www.amazon.com)
Amazon can be difficult to navigate if you are not sure what you want. But if you are looking for a specific, brand-named item (such as Crayola crayons), I find that Amazon often has the most reasonably priced options. We purchase our water beads from Amazon as well as many science supplies, such as color tablets.

Discount School Supply (http://www.discountschoolsupply.com)
This site has a huge selection of art and craft supplies. We stock up on large rolls of kraft paper for protecting our art area, BioColor paint, all types of art paper, and fun painting tools. Discount School Supply is a good source for science supplies too, including materials such as graduated cylinders or fake snow.

Etsy (http://www.etsy.com)
If you can't find something on Amazon, you can probably find someone to make it for you on Etsy. We purchase all kinds of items through Etsy, but we consistently rely on Etsy sellers for wood craft supplies, beads, cutouts, and so on. Some items can be expensive, but it's worth checking!

Kaplan Early Learning Company (www.kaplanco.com)
In the interest of full disclosure, this is the parent company of my publisher, but I wanted to include them because they have a huge selection of play and arts and crafts materials. We are big fans of Sargent Art's liquid watercolors and glitter glue, which they carry. And for those who are mess-averse (you know who you are!), Kaplan has a great selection of aprons and mats to help keep your kiddos and their play area clean. You can search for products by age too, which is helpful for parents looking for materials for younger children.

The Land of Nod (http://www.landofnod.com)
I have been a contributor to the Land of Nod's blog for a few years, and I was a customer of the brand long before that. They have great craft kits, but I love their large art supply box and fabulously colored felt markers. And they are my go-to for well-made furniture and organization items perfect for any kids' activity area. In addition, you can find plenty of celebration supplies at Nod.

Munchkin (http://www.munchkin.com)
Munchkin is an occasional sponsor of content on my blog and a maker of fun, fabulously designed products for babies and kids. It's probably not one you would think of for art and craft supplies, but I love reusing their colorful plastic ware for art and craft projects. The tableware items are sturdy and safe, and kids like the bright colors.

Oriental Trading Company (http://www.orientaltrading.com)
This is an inexpensive place to shop for fun seasonal items and reasonably priced craft kits. I've found their everyday art paper selection to be on par with other suppliers.

School Specialty (https://store.schoolspecialty.com)
School Specialty tends to carry higher-quality (and thus higher-priced) art products, but that includes our favorite (and in my opinion, totally worth it) Sax tempera paint cakes. They also have a good selection of craft supplies.

MAJOR CHAIN STORES

If you are the type of person who really needs to see art and craft supplies in person or your children can actually keep from throwing a tantrum about not buying everything, there are several major chain stores I'd recommend. It's also definitely worth noting that many of these stores frequently have excellent sales and clearance shelves, and you can usually find coupons floating around. Make sure to check!

A.C. Moore (http://www.acmoore.com)
A large store filled with all the arts and crafts you could want.

IKEA (http://www.ikea.com)
IKEA has a limited selection, but great art supplies. We love their tempera paint cakes and packaged art paper. And they have a great basic, inexpensive easel.

Michaels (http://www.michaels.com)
These stores tend to stock supplies for a range of arts and crafts activities.

Target (http://www.target.com)
Target carries popular brand names in kids' art supplies (such as Crayola) as well as its own brand. I have been happy and impressed with the great selection of Kid Made Modern art projects and supplies.

In addition to the stores listed above, your local grocery store will have the household items you need for many of your in-home science projects, including dry ice. If you can't find dry ice at your local grocery store but are intent on the cool experiment, check with a local ice and beverage supplier or seafood store to see if they will sell it to you.

THRIFT STORES

Thrift stores can be overwhelming, and often require time and patience to peruse the selection. Thus, they are not usually my favorite stores for supplies. But occasionally the kids and I are up for an adventure, and we'll head to a thrift store to see if we can find any good treasures.

Check the kids' section for art and craft supplies as well as the home goods section for tools you might be able to use in your projects (for example, potato mashers for stamping projects or playdough fun). The availability of thrift stores will obviously vary by your location, and many are run by local charitable organizations. I've found these stores in most metropolitan areas:

AMVETS (http://www.amvetsnsf.org/stores.html)

Goodwill (http://www.goodwill.org)

The Salvation Army (http://www.salvationarmyusa.org)

Savers (http://www.savers.com)

Value Village (http://www.valuevillage.com)

You can search online to find a thrift store located near you. And of course, you will have your own preferences about which organizations you do or do not want to support with your business.

OUTDOOR ORGANIZATIONS

If you're looking for a new local outdoor spot to play or you're planning to travel and are researching for your trip, I highly recommend starting with the National Park Service (NPS). You can find national parks all over the country—many of which you may not know exist and are likely close by. As I mentioned, we are big fans of the NPS Junior Ranger program and are always on the hunt for new national parks to visit. Check out the NPS website (http://www.nps.gov) to help locate a park near you and get all the information you need on family programming offered.

In addition to the NPS, check out your local parks and recreation department. We love discovering new local parks, and I'm always amazed at the programming available through parks and recreation departments. Many of the events are not widely advertised, so it pays to look. Local parks and rec organizations are also a good place to investigate community gardens and other environmental stewardship programs. These are all great ways to get the kids outside!

If you're interested in getting your family in the competitive spirit and trying out a kids' obstacle race, check out these options:

Down & Dirty Obstacle Race (http://www.downanddirtyobstaclerace.com/adventure-kids/)

Fruit Shoot Mini Mudder (https://toughmudder.com/fruit-shoot-mini-mudder)

Spartan Kids (http://www.spartankids.com)

And last, but not least, look for local nature blogs! Even if they're not specific to kids or family activities, you'll find plenty of nature blogs that can help identify good hiking spots, nature centers, and local outdoor activities. (The Natural Capital is our favorite local nature blog: http://www.thenaturalcapital.com.) Bloggers are a great resource for local information and you should use them!

NATIONAL MUSEUM ORGANIZATIONS

Most major museums belong to one national organization or another for their particular category. I've found these organizations to be a great starting point for two things: to help locate a type of museum (either locally or nationally when we travel), and as a valuable provider of reciprocal membership. Museum membership can be expensive, but if the museum is a member of a national organization, it's likely that a membership to one museum will earn you some type of reciprocal membership at other museums within that organization. The type and value of reciprocity is determined by each museum, so make sure to check. I have always found that if we plan to take our entire family and a few guests to a type of museum at least twice per year, the membership is worth it. For example, one year we joined the Port Discovery Children's Museum in Baltimore. Even though we only visited that actual museum once, we also received reciprocal admission at the Chicago Children's Museum and the Children's Museum of Richmond. You may find that the membership is worth it and helps you avoid forcing your kids to stay and get a day's worth of play out of an expensive admission ticket. Many museums have national organizations, but we use the following ones the most:

American Alliance of Museums (http://www.aam-us.org)

Association of Children's Museums (http://www.childrensmuseums.org)

Association of Science-Technology Centers (http://www.astc.org)

Association of Zoos and Aquariums (http://www.aza.org)

OTHER ACTIVITY BLOGS

It's no big surprise that I rely heavily on family-friendly blogs to find fun and educational activities for our kids. I happen to have a bias toward my own Not-So-SAHM blog, but you should definitely spend a little time looking for your favorites. Often, one good find leads you to others, as blogs link to and coordinate with other like-minded blogs. Each one has its own focus and style, so look for one that appeals most to you. Here is just a small selection of my daily reads:

Art Bar Blog (http://www.artbarblog.com)

The Artful Parent (http://www.artfulparent.com)

The Crafty Crow (http://www.thecraftycrow.net)

Hello, Wonderful (http://www.hellowonderful.co)

Honest to Nod (http://blog.landofnod.com)

KidFriendly DC (http://www.kidfriendlydc.com)

Meri Cherry (http://www.mericherry.com)

Modern Parents Messy Kids (http://www.modernparentsmessykids.com)

No Monsters in My Bed (http://www.bedtimemonsters.blogspot.com)

Tinkerlab (http://www.tinkerlab.com)

INDEX